Landmark
B O O K S

The Pirate Lafitte
and the
Battle of New Orleans

Landmark

B O O K S

THE
PIRATE
LAFITTE

and the Battle of
New Orleans

BY ROBERT TALLANT

illustrated by JOHN CHASE

RANDOM HOUSE · NEW YORK

ACKNOWLEDGMENTS

Many sources were consulted during the preparation of this book, for numerous New Orleans and Louisiana authors have told some of the Jean Lafitte stories in past years. Perhaps the best known of these is *Lafitte the Pirate*, by Lyle Saxon, a rich and colorful account of the Lafittes and their period, a book to which I am indebted. Other Louisiana writers whose works I consulted include Charles Gayarré, Grace King, Henry C. Castellanos, Eliza Ripley, and Ray M. Thompson.

ROBERT TALLANT

New Orleans
1951

Contents

1: The Last Pirate

YOUNG ESAU GLASSCOCK WAS EXCITED. HE
had looked forward to this moment for days.
Now that Morgan and Blackbeard had vanished from the seas, he knew that Jean Lafitte
was the only well-known pirate alive. At least
Esau had heard many wild tales which seemed to
prove that Lafitte was a pirate.

It was on a warm November day in 1809
that Esau had an opportunity to learn for him-

self if the tales were true. On that afternoon he went with his father to the Lafitte cottage on St. Philip Street in New Orleans.

The cottage was small and on one side there was a garden behind a wall in which a gate was set. Esau's heart beat fast as Mr. Glasscock raised the knocker on the gate and then let it fall.

In a moment a dark woman opened the gate. Bowing pleasantly, she led Esau and his father to some chairs placed among the oleanders and banana trees. Although the woman chattered as she walked, Esau couldn't understand a word of what his father and she were saying. He knew only that they were speaking in French.

"Is he here, Father?" Esau asked, as the woman vanished into the little house.

Mr. Glasscock smiled. "Don't be too disappointed, Esau," he said, knowing how much the boy had wanted to meet Jean Lafitte. "We are to talk to Pierre Lafitte. Jean Lafitte is not here."

Esau was a little disappointed, although it could have been worse. If it were true that Jean was a pirate, then his brother Pierre must be one, too, since they were engaged in the same activities. But it was Jean who was the leader, and it was he whom Esau had hoped to see. The king of the buccaneers!

A short, heavyset man came out of the house and approached the two visitors. "I'm Lafitte," he said quite simply. Then shaking hands with Esau and Mr. Glasscock, he sat down. In a few minutes the dark woman brought out steaming cups of coffee.

While the older men talked, Esau studied Pierre Lafitte. He was about thirty, with fair hair and a big, genial smile. He did not look as fierce as Esau had imagined a pirate might look. Nevertheless, he was strong, and something about his eyes made Esau feel that he would not like Pierre Lafitte to be angry with him.

In answer to Mr. Glasscock's questions, Pierre said that Jean Lafitte was down in the Baratarian swamps below New Orleans, and would not be back for at least a week. "But I'm sure we can get you six likely blacks," said Pierre, slapping his knee vigorously.

"I'll have to go down there then," Mr. Glasscock said. "I'm in a hurry to get back to the plantation. Is it possible to arrange for a guide?"

"That can be arranged," Pierre Lafitte assured him.

"It becomes more difficult every day for a man to buy slaves," said Mr. Glasscock.

This talk of slaves was not new to Esau. Everyone he knew owned Negroes, and there had been slaves in his family ever since he could remember. Back home in Virginia his father had owned many slaves. Now that Mr. Glasscock had moved with his wife and two sons to a plantation in Louisiana, not far from New Orleans, he needed many more slaves to work the fields. Esau knew that even George Washington had owned slaves, and so did that other great Virginian, Thomas Jefferson. It was a custom of the time.

But recently the United States had placed an embargo on the importation of any more Negroes from Africa, for even in 1809 many people were beginning to be opposed to slavery. Since then planters in the South had found it difficult to get new field hands. That was why Mr. Glasscock and Esau had come down to New Orleans. Mr. Glasscock had been told there was to be an auction in the city of a large number of slaves. Then, at the last moment, something had gone wrong and the sale had been canceled. It was this that had sent them to the Lafittes. Everyone said that the Lafittes could sell you slaves when no one else could.

Esau listened while his father completed arrangements to leave the next morning for the Barataria swamps. When the Glasscocks left the cottage and were walking through the narrow streets of old New Orleans Esau began to worry. He had heard a lot about the dangers of Barataria.

All that country from New Orleans down to the Gulf of Mexico, to Grand Isle, Grande Terre and Chênière Caminada—the three major settlements in the wild and treacherous swamps —was a mystery to most people. True, there were said to be natives of the region who could find their way through the narrow bayous as easily as other men walked along city streets. But it was different in the case of a stranger.

People had vanished forever among the murky waters, the tall grass, the jungle of queerly twisted trees, and were never seen or heard of again. Some were said to have died of fever and hunger. Others were believed to have been set upon and murdered for the very clothes on their backs, for the region was infested not only by snakes, alligators and mosquitoes, but also by all kinds of outlaws—criminals, half-insane runaway slaves, smugglers and pirates.

But his father laughed when Esau spoke of his fears.

"There's nothing to worry about, Esau," Mr. Glasscock said. "I'll be in very good hands. The Lafittes and I have business together and they'll look out for me. Besides, I've heard that Jean Lafitte lives very handsomely down there. Don't believe everything you hear."

This almost made Esau forget his worry, for he became excited again about Jean Lafitte. "May I come with you?" he asked.

"You had better stay here," his father replied. "I'll only be gone a few days, and you'll find lots of things in New Orleans to amuse you."

Esau argued, for not only did he want to see Jean Lafitte, but he felt that it would be easier to be with his father in whatever dangers he met than to stay behind worrying in the city. But his father's mind could not be changed.

The Glasscocks were guests of John Randolph Grymes, a young lawyer, also a Virginian, who had come to New Orleans in search of adventure and to establish himself in the practice of law. He was only twenty-four in 1809, but he was already making money and becoming famous in the city. Among his friends was Governor W. C. C. Claiborne, another Virginian, who had been appointed governor of Louisiana after the United States purchased Louisiana from France in 1803.

The friendship between Mr. Glasscock and Mr. Grymes was an old one, for Mr. Glasscock had known the lawyer as a boy back home in Virginia. Because of this, Mr. Grymes had insisted that Esau and his father make his home theirs during their visit in New Orleans.

Esau was awake and dressed when his father departed for the swamps at dawn the next morning. Two swarthy men had appeared on horseback and Mr. Grymes had had another horse ready and saddled for Mr. Glasscock. Esau knew they would travel only a small part of the way by horseback and that then they would take to the narrow streams called "bayous" in little boats. Despite his troubled mind, Esau tingled with excitement. When the party rode off and the sounds of the horses' hoofs grew thinner over the cobblestones, he turned to Mr. Grymes. "Are those men pirates, too?" he asked.

Mr. Grymes shrugged his shoulders and laughed. "Some people would say they are and some that they are not, Esau," he said. Then he added, "Your father will be safe."

"What do the Lafittes really do?" Esau asked.

"Many things," Mr. Grymes said. "For one thing, they have a blacksmith shop on St. Philip and Bourbon Streets, just across from the cottage where you and your father met Pierre Lafitte. They also have a shop on Royal Street, where they sell a lot of merchandise to people in the city. It is true they deal in slaves, too, but so do others, and the best citizens in the city do business with them. Some of the finest men in New Orleans are their friends."

Esau was puzzled, for he had expected to find that the Lafittes' reputations would be much worse than this. "Then why does Jean Lafitte hide out at Barataria?" he asked.

"He doesn't hide out," Mr. Grymes said. "He has a home on Grande Terre. Some of his business is conducted from there. I assure you he can be seen on the streets of New Orleans and in the coffee houses any time he is in the city."

Once more Esau felt keen disappointment. It was just his luck that Jean Lafitte was not in the city now! Any other time he might have seen him.

During the next few days Esau walked about New Orleans, exploring the city, sometimes with Mr. Grymes and sometimes alone. He thought the city was the strangest place he had ever seen, with its narrow streets and its foreign-looking buildings. Most of the buildings were flush with the sidewalks and decorated with balconies and iron lacework. It did not look like an American city at all, Esau thought, but more like pictures he had seen of cities in France and in Spain. Then he remembered that New Orleans had only become an American city six years ago, in 1803. Even then it was already old, for his father had told him New Orleans had been founded in 1718.

Not even the language he heard in the streets was English. Most of the people spoke French, although sometimes Esau recognized some words he heard as Spanish. Once in a while he would ask someone on the street a question. Often he found that the person could not understand him. Mr. Grymes said that some day all the people in New Orleans would be speaking English as did all other Americans, but Esau found this hard to believe. He had learned that most of the people called themselves Creoles and did not even like Americans very much.

Esau thought New Orleans was both very dirty and very beautiful. The gutters were almost always filled with stagnant water and those streets that were not paved with cobblestones were muddy and scarred with deep, soggy holes. On the other hand, many of the brick houses were painted soft pinks and blues, and most of these were decorated with delicate iron lacework that had been made by slaves. All over the city were gardens filled with beautiful and strange flowers and shrubs that Esau had never seen back home in Virginia.

Mr. Grymes took him to the French Market, and he enjoyed the colorful people he saw on every side. In the crowds were black people in their gaudy finery, most of the women with their heads wrapped in bright cloths. There were Indians, too, who sat outside, wrapped in red and blue and yellow blankets, selling herbs and handwoven baskets. It was all different from anything he had ever seen.

Yet as the days went on Esau grew more impatient for his father's return, despite the fact that Mr. Grymes kept telling him not to worry. "Your father will be back any day now," the lawyer said again and again.

Esau imagined all sorts of things. What might not happen to his father down there after all? "Perhaps those men have taken him to Grand Isle for some evil reason," Esau said to Mr. Grymes. "How can they be trusted?"

Then Mr. Grymes, perhaps impatient, looked at him and said, "If you are really that upset, Esau, you might visit Pierre Lafitte."

"That's exactly what I'm going to do," Esau said, realizing that he had been wanting to do that for several days now.

So the next day he went back to the Lafitte cottage. The dark woman opened the gate and recognized him at once. "He's in the blacksmith shop," she told him, in broken English.

Esau thanked her and walked across the street in the direction in which she had pointed. The blacksmith shop was a low, one-story building with a gently sloping roof, and Esau felt his heart beat faster as he approached it. After all, this was rumored to be one of the places where the pirates held their secret meetings. Esau imagined the little building looked sinister, but he swung open a door and went in.

At first he could hardly see inside. The great forge in the center of the room was blazing high and beyond the fire there was only dense blackness. Then, as his eyes became adjusted to the darkness, he saw two men sitting at a wooden table near the forge. One of them was Pierre Lafitte, the other was older and larger.

At the sound of footsteps, Pierre turned and saw his young visitor. "Hallo!" the man shouted. Rising from his seat, he approached Esau.

Now that he was here, the boy felt embarrassed but Pierre slapped him on the back heartily. "Come over by the fire," Pierre said. "It is cold outside today."

Lafitte introduced the other man as "old Thiac." Old Thiac, he explained, in hesitant but understandable English, had a forge near the levee that ran along the edge of the Mississippi River, and he sometimes came to visit.

"We do not do much business here, do we, old Thiac?" he said and laughed loudly.

Esau thought to himself that they did not seem to do any business, at least as blacksmiths. Except for the forge and some blacksmith's instruments lying about he could see no evidence of real work.

"And what can I do for you?" Pierre Lafitte wanted to know.

Esau asked him if he had any word about his father.

"It is not easy to get word from down there," Lafitte said. Then, seeming to sense that Esau was disturbed about his father, Pierre put an arm around the boy's shoulder and began to reassure him. "Your father is probably having a good time," he said. "My brother is a fine host. True enough, the trip through the swamps may be long and dangerous, but not for those who know it as we do."

"My father has been gone a long time," Esau explained.

"He will be home tomorrow or the next day," Pierre answered confidently. "You will see."

Esau did feel better as he walked back to

the home of Mr. Grymes. "Pierre Lafitte knows that Father will be back within a day or two," thought Esau. "I'm sure of it."

When he awakened the next morning he was strangely certain that his father had already returned. Dressing hurriedly, Esau rushed downstairs. There was his father having breakfast with Mr. Grymes!

Mr. Glasscock looked happy and healthy and he was filled with tales of his adventures. Captain Jean Lafitte, he told Esau and Mr. Grymes, had treated him as if he were a king. He had enjoyed the finest food and wines, and the village at Grande Terre was overflowing with treasures. Indeed, the place was quite different from what he had expected. It was a kind of wild Paradise, and the swamps of Barataria were indescribably beautiful.

Esau wanted most to hear about Jean Lafitte.

"Why, he is a fine French gentleman," said Mr. Glasscock. "A strong man with a fiery disposition perhaps, but with an equally strong character and good manners."

After telling Mr. Grymes how Lafitte had supplied the needed slaves, Mr. Glasscock turned back to Esau and winked. "You can

make up your own mind about Jean Lafitte,"
he said. "We are all invited to a ball tonight.
You will meet him there."

All that day Esau was tormented by suspense,
but at last evening came and he set out with
his father for the building where the ball was
being held. It was only a few blocks from the
home of Mr. Grymes.

Once inside Esau knew he had never seen
such a sight. The rooms glowed with candlelight, and the music of violins filled them with
music. Beautifully dressed women moved about
on the arms of tall, gallant men, any of whom,
Esau thought for a few moments, might be Jean
Lafitte. Negro servants passed trays of refresh-
ments.

Then a young man stepped out of the crowd
and came forward to greet Mr. Glasscock and
Mr. Grymes. Suddenly Esau felt his own hand
grasped in a grip of steel. The strange man
said a few words and moved away to greet other
friends. "That was he!" exclaimed Esau.

"Yes, that was Jean Lafitte," said Mr. Grymes,
laughing at Esau's excitement.

Esau could not go to sleep that night until
he had written a letter to Ned, his brother.

Dear Brother Ned, he wrote, *I have
seen the notorious Captain Lafitte ...*

He paused and wondered why he had used
that word "notorious." Was it because he knew
the Lafitte blacksmith shop was no blacksmith
shop at all, and that there was more mystery
about the Lafittes than either his father or Mr.
Grymes would tell him?

Esau went on writing, describing Jean Lafitte:

*He is tall, with pale skin, and he has
large black eyes. He is clean-shaven
except for a beard extending part-way
down his cheeks. He greeted our father
as an old friend ...*

He wrote more, telling Ned about how their
father had made the trip to Grand Isle and
Grande Terre to buy the slaves from Jean
Lafitte. Esau added that he and his father would
start for home the next day on the steamboat.

This letter was a very real one, just as Esau
Glasscock was a real youth. The letter still exists
in a library in New Orleans.

2: The Mystery of Jean Lafitte

Esau glasscock's description of Jean
Lafitte in his letter to Ned is as good as any
we have. Of course there are others. He is
described as having been as slim and strong as
the rapier with which he fought his duels. His
eyes are always said to have been black and
fierce. There are even portraits in New Orleans
which are said to be of Lafitte, but none of
them has ever been proven to bear an exact

likeness to the pirate who became a great patriot.

For mystery must forever surround Jean Lafitte and his brother, Pierre. We know some of the deeds they performed. We know all the important ones. We know many details of their characters. Yet we do not really know who they were or even where they came from before they appeared in New Orleans.

The stories that sound the truest state that they were Frenchmen who came from France by way of the West Indies. Some writers have thought that both brothers had served with Napoleon in his wars. Others think it was only Pierre who had seen battle, and that he had been in the French Navy. Jean must have been about fourteen years old during the Reign of Terror that followed the French Revolution. He may have run away from France at that time.

Jean Lafitte first appeared in New Orleans in about 1803, the year of the Louisiana Purchase. He was twenty-four years old then and Pierre was a year or two older. Yet, although Jean was the younger brother, he seems always to have been the leader of the two Lafittes.

Pierre Lafitte was the more even-tempered of

the two. He was affable and often jolly. Jean Lafitte was hot-tempered and quick to use sword or pistol. He was an expert duelist. It was known that he had killed a man in a duel in Charleston. He smiled rarely.

Yet Jean Lafitte never fought unless it was for a purpose in which he believed. During his first years in New Orleans he went about with the Creole gentlemen of the city. He never took part in brawls among the rough men with whom he sometimes associated, many of whom were shady individuals from all parts of the world and of all bloods and nationalities. He was educated, spoke several languages, and, as Esau's father remarked, had elegant manners. It was these qualities that brought him into the best circles in New Orleans. It was said that once a person had met Jean Lafitte it was impossible to believe that he was a pirate, a buccaneer.

The truth is that he was not a pirate at first. When he and Pierre first settled in New Orleans they were privateers. Pirates and privateers were quite different. A pirate headed a band of men on his own ship or ships and attacked any vessel at sea in search of booty and treasure. A privateer was usually in the pay of some country at war with another country, and only the ships of the enemy country were attacked. Few people of that period thought of a privateer as a criminal, but piracy was a crime punishable by death and the pirate was considered the most evil of men.

A privateer held a peculiar document called a letter of marque. Jean Lafitte had a letter of marque from Cartagena, a seaport of Colombia, which had declared itself independent of Spain and was at war with Spain when Lafitte began his activities. Jean Lafitte hated Spain. It is said that he told a number of people, "I will be at war with Spain all my life."

According to the beliefs of his time, the letter of marque gave Lafitte the "right" to attack and loot Spanish ships whenever and wherever he pleased. In a sense he was fighting for Cartagena. In reality, as a Frenchman, he was fighting for France against her old enemy, Spain, and for himself.

France at that time was granting letters of marque, too, with Spain's commerce the prey of the privateers to whom the letters of marque were granted. Why Lafitte chose Colombia's letter rather than one from France remains one of the mysteries about him. Perhaps he was not in such good standing with the French government. Perhaps Colombia and Cartagena were closer and it was easier to get the letter there. Perhaps the new Colombian government at Cartagena approached him and suggested that he become one of their privateers. Perhaps he decided that this would be an excellent way to fight Spain.

As Jean Lafitte was called a pirate long before he even possibly became one, so he was also called a smuggler. In those early years he did not engage in smuggling himself, but he did act as an agent for men who were probably smugglers. There were many smugglers at Barataria and many merchants and other people in New Orleans who wanted the goods they could get in no other way but from the Baratarians. The most respectable citizens of New Orleans did business with them. The New Orleans historian, Grace King, wrote: "In the old French colonial days the uncertainty of supplies from the mother country had rendered it (smuggling) almost a necessity of existence."

So there had been smuggling in the swamplands below New Orleans for at least fifty years

before Jean Lafitte ever saw the country. Jean
Lafitte organized the smuggling and gradually
became its leader until, finally, almost all buyers
of smuggled merchandise had to conduct their
business through Lafitte.

At the time that Esau Glasscock met the
Lafittes they seem to have been leading quiet
and peaceful lives, running their business exactly as if it were any lawful trade. The people
of New Orleans thought no less of them for it.
Most of the population of the city was French
and Spanish or a blending of the two. Legally
New Orleans was part of the United States, but
the citizens had not taken it seriously yet, and
when they thought about it they resented it.
They did not like the new laws nor care much
for the new government or for Governor Claiborne.

From 1803 until 1810 the Lafittes led undis-
turbed lives. They conducted most of their
business from the blacksmith forge on St. Philip
Street and the shop on Royal Street. It was said
that the Royal Street shop was backed financially
by some of the rich men of the city.

Both the Lafittes made frequent trips from
the city to the Gulf of Mexico. They traveled

the gulf islands and came back with black slaves and rich merchandise which could be bought from no one else, and which were quickly sold.

Now and then someone whispered the word "pirates," but no one seems to have cared except a few of the new Americans in the city, such as William C. C. Claiborne. The other people of New Orleans shrugged their shoulders at these accusations. "The Americans should mind their business!" they said. Smuggling had been going on a long time. It was a custom and a habit. Under Spanish rule, tariffs had made the prices of necessary goods too high. Only by smuggling what they needed could Orleanians live. It would always go on, people thought. How else could a man get slaves? Or the rich silks for his wife's beautiful dresses? Besides, smuggled goods were much cheaper than those imported from Europe in the regular way.

But all did not go smoothly for the Lafittes all the time. For instance, in 1810 there was a bloody war at Barataria. Two groups not yet under Lafitte control reached a state of feud. The trouble began when one group raided a ship of the other that was returning from a voyage to the African coast. The vessel was loaded with Negroes to be sold in New Orleans, possibly by the Lafittes. After the attack, the ship was never seen again, for it was probably scuttled and sunk, but the captured Negroes showed up at the warehouse or "barracoon" at Barataria.

The feud raged all the summer of 1810. Members of the two groups of smugglers fought to the death on sight. Armed with knives and guns they stalked the marshes searching for each other. The disorder threatened to ruin the whole business of smuggling and privateering.

It was Jean Lafitte who settled the trouble. He called the leaders of each group together, and tried to bring them to a peaceful understanding. When the **discussion** was over the groups were welded into one and into Lafitte's own strange republic. Thus Jean Lafitte increased his own power.

For it did become a sort of republic he ruled. Perhaps it was really a kingdom. Jean Lafitte ruled as a king and lived like one. Although he was fair and just in settling the disputes that arose among his Baratarians, his word and his final decisions were law. All Barataria was under his control—privateers, smugglers, trappers, fishermen. He had won his position by his quick intelligence and his physical strength, and some-times with money, for he had a great deal of money, as well as rich supporters in New Orleans.

He had, as has been said, always been the leader even over his brother, Pierre. In 1810, which seems to have been Jean's first important year, even this was strengthened. For that year Pierre had a stroke of apoplexy. He recovered, but he never again looked as he had when Esau met him. His eyes remained slightly crossed and this gave him a strange, fierce look he had never had before. If Esau had seen him after his ill-ness he would have thought Pierre Lafitte did look like a pirate. Pierre's health does not seem to have been as good as before, either. He seemed glad to let Jean Lafitte take over more and more authority and to remain the leader of their band of men.

Thus did Jean Lafitte come into complete power. In 1810 he could not have known how important his future was to be, or the part he was to play in American history within the next few years. Until now, he must have been in-terested only in acquiring wealth and power for himself—and perhaps in making the commerce of Spain difficult. If he had patriotism it was probably for France, not for the United States. He would have laughed if he had been told he was to play an important role in saving New Orleans for America.

To the people of New Orleans Jean Lafitte was still a mystery. He was young, strong, handsome, and dashing. The mystery surrounding him made him more interesting. He brought the city folk what they needed and wanted, and they paid him for it. He grew richer and more powerful every year. He was a familiar sight on the streets, but people never stopped staring at him with curiosity. They whispered that he was a pirate and then that he did not look in the least like a pirate. No one was ever sure whether he was or not.

There is one thing of which we can be sure. Jean Lafitte hated the word. Over and over again he denied it. "My men are privateers," he said. "They are corsairs, not pirates."

Yet the word continued to be used. People whispered that the Baratarians brought in many contraband ships, much booty, thousands of slaves. But they never took a prisoner. What became of the crews of the captured ships? they asked. Had they walked a gangplank and fallen into the ocean never to be seen again, as had the victims of pirates for centuries?

So there were always people who, when Jean Lafitte passed them in the streets, pointed him out to strangers and said, "That is Jean Lafitte the pirate!"

There were many duels..

3: Old New Orleans

NEW ORLEANS WAS A STRANGE CITY IN the days of Jean Lafitte. It was nothing like any American city. It was quite different from the New Orleans of today. Although it was small, it was already very old. To understand Lafitte and the conditions that existed we must know a little about the city and its story.

New Orleans was founded by Jean Baptiste Le Moyne de Bienville, a French soldier, around 1718. Later, in 1723, it became the capital of the huge colonial empire called Louisiana. For fifty years after its beginning New Orleans was

French. Most of the people had come from France. They spoke French and their customs and habits were French.

Distances were great in those days and the people of the tiny capital were almost entirely cut off from other parts of the North American continent. The citizens of New Orleans had little or no interest in what was going on in New England. Even when the American Revolution broke out New Orleans knew little about it and had no interest in it. Americans were strangers and foreigners. Orleanians were colonial Frenchmen.

During those first fifty years the citizens of New Orleans had more contact with France than with any other country. When they traveled it was to France. They sent their children to France to be educated. The ships that came up the Mississippi River from the Gulf of Mexico brought mostly French people. These new arrivals were coming to make their homes and fortunes in Louisiana, to settle in the city or on the land surrounding it.

All kinds of people came, adventurers and soldiers, aristocrats and criminals, priests and nuns. There were also many ordinary people, who simply wanted to go into business, to farm, to trap, to do anything that would earn them a living in the New World. They found it would not be too easy. There were Indians to fight, unhealthful climatic conditions to be overcome, even wild animals to be driven away. In the end all this was conquered. The newcomers from France had founded a city.

By 1769 New Orleans had a population of about 5000, including whites, Indians, and Negroes. It was a little town situated on the banks of the Mississippi River, almost all of it in what is still called the French Quarter. But there were schools and a church and even a theater where plays were given. New Orleans was already a civilized city. Then what seemed a dreadful thing to the French citizens of New Orleans occurred. They discovered that France had sold Louisiana to Spain.

The actual transfer had taken place six years before, but it was not until 1769 that the Spanish arrived in force to take over the city. One day twenty-four Spanish men-of-war appeared at the mouth of the river and word spread that they were coming to occupy the city with Spanish soldiers. There was tremendous tumult and excitement and the men of New Orleans banded together to resist the invasion. This made the city the first place in America to revolt against rule by a European power. But the resistance amounted to nothing.

The Spanish arrived in August and took possession at once. The twelve leaders of the citizens who had met in October of the year before to demand the expulsion of Don Antonio de Ulloa, the Spanish commissioner, were thrown into prison. Later six of them were executed. The Spanish general, Count Alexander O'Reilly, sometimes called "Bloody" O'Reilly, replaced the French flag in the parade grounds, called the Place d'Armes, with the flag of Spain. New Orleans was now a Spanish city.

New Orleans did not like it, but Spanish rule proved to be milder than had been feared. Spanish soldiers married New Orleans girls. Soon French New Orleans seems to have absorbed the Spanish. The law might now be Spanish, but French customs were still the rule. It was the French language that was most often heard on the streets and in gatherings.

The strictest of the Spanish laws were those that had to do with trade. Smuggling, always present, had become widespread. It was fun to fool the Spanish authorities. This was long before Jean Lafitte arrived in the city. Even then Barataria was filled with smugglers, privateers who raided Spanish ships, sinister groups of men who could offer merchandise it was impossible to buy in the city.

In 1788 real disaster struck New Orleans. Almost the entire town was destroyed by a fire that broke out on Good Friday of that year. But it was rebuilt at once, this time of stone and brick instead of the wood that had been used before. One of the few buildings to survive the fire was the little structure that was to become the blacksmith shop of the brothers Lafitte.

In 1794 there was another large fire, although not as bad a one as the first. Again the future blacksmith shop survived. It seemed to be waiting for Jean and Pierre Lafitte.

Louisiana became a French possession again in 1801. Spain, having little use for the colony and finding its administration difficult and expensive, traded it to Napoleon Bonaparte for a part of Italy. Napoleon kept this secret for a long time. He was at war with England and he did not want it known that Louisiana was again

French. When the bargain was made public the people of New Orleans were not too happy. It meant another change of laws and money, from Spanish back to French.

Then in 1803, Napoleon, in need of money, sold Louisiana to the United States. Governor Claiborne arrived to take charge. For all general purposes New Orleans was an American city, although Louisiana was not admitted to state-hood until 1812.

The people of New Orleans resented the Louisiana Purchase more than any other change they had experienced. The citizens of French and Spanish blood, by now called Creoles, dis-liked Claiborne and all Americans. They hated the new customs, the new laws. They refused to learn English. There were constant duels be-tween Creoles and Americans. Signs and plac-ards denouncing the Americans were nailed up at night, to be discovered in the mornings.

The Americans did not like the older resi-dents of New Orleans much either. The new Americans found New Orleans like a foreign city. Its customs and habits were different from those of New England, New York or Virginia. They thought the people lazy and lawless.

Among the things they could not understand was the dealing with the smugglers. Yet it was not long before many Americans were also doing business with them.

Those who did not follow this practice were bitter about people who did. By 1810 and even before, they were saying that Lafitte should be in jail instead of being treated with respect and regard, as if he were a hero of some kind. They whispered all kinds of things. They all felt they knew what must go on down at Barataria, at Grand Isle and at Grande Terre.

Governor Claiborne was one of these. He did not approve of smuggling or of privateering. He did not approve of Jean Lafitte. He called the Baratarians pirates in plain and simple language.

4: The Barataria Hideouts

PEOPLE HAD BEEN LIVING ALONG THE BARA-
taria waterways, at Grand Isle and at Grande
Terre long before Lafitte was born. Most of
them were Spanish, Portuguese and French, but
there were men of every race and nationality.
They lived in small villages and groups and in
families, as people do everywhere. Most of them
had wives and children. The men fished and
trapped and took part in smuggling. Some
followed all three occupations, for they considered smuggling as normal a trade as fishing
and trapping.

Many of them worked for Jean Lafitte after he arrived in the region and as his power increased. To be sure Lafitte had his own band of men, some of whom had come from all parts of the world, but he engaged the native Baratarians when he needed them. They thought of him as a friend, as well as their leader. He was fair in his dealings. If a man lost an arm or a leg or an eye Jean Lafitte paid him an extra sum of money. If he were killed Lafitte saw to it that his family received help.

These were simple people, most of them religious and kind. Of course there were real criminals in the swamps, men hiding from the law. But these seldom caused trouble. The Baratarians minded their business. If a real badman did start any trouble they had their own ways of handling him. The swamp kept its secrets.

By 1811 Jean Lafitte was living on Grande Terre whenever he was not in New Orleans. His house was the largest on the island and furnished with fine carpets, silver, glassware and other articles that were the booty of Spanish ships. Here he entertained visitors from New

Orleans and made bargains for the sale of his merchandise. Next to his home was the warehouse, brimming with articles he had to sell. Behind that was the barracoon of the slaves.

On warm afternoons when Lafitte wasn't busy he could lie in a hammock on his wide porch and watch the bright sails of his fleet not far away. About him spread the palmetto-thatched roofs of the huts where the men closest to him lived. He was powerful now, rich and proud.

Of course Grande Terre was only a small part of his kingdom, the capital as it were. There were other warehouses and other men on Grand Isle and at Chênière Caminada, and all the way from the Gulf of Mexico, through the winding bayous, to New Orleans. Booty was hidden in a dozen spots, closely guarded by trusted men. It was all his—the wild swampland, the wealth, the people.

Lafitte could laugh at the American Governor, Claiborne, who was beginning to threaten him now. There was not a Baratarian who would not fight for him. Let any enemy of Lafitte's invade this kingdom and signals would pass through it from one end to the other, warning him of danger. Not that he feared Claiborne. Did he not still walk all over New Orleans, visit the blacksmith shop, the Royal Street shop, and the coffee houses? No one had yet dared to touch him.

Men often came down to buy slaves from Lafitte. Some of these he received at Grande Terre, but others he met in certain places half-way between the Gulf of Mexico and the city. The most important of these was on a *chênière* called The Temple.

A *chênière* is really a kind of island in the Louisiana swamps. In traveling from New Orleans to the Gulf of Mexico, across what is still called a "trembling prairie" it is necessary to follow one curving stream after another, bayous that widen into lakes, then become narrow again. No one can ever be sure where the water ends and the land begins. Everything is green and a misty blue, and tall grasses higher than a man's head obscure the land. Baratarians know their way about as you know the streets of your town, but a stranger can still be lost forever in all this green and blue and golden landscape. Yet here and there are the *chênières,* islands of white shells, usually covered with gigantic oak trees.

In Lafitte's day The Temple was one of the largest of these. It was a fantastic place where giant oaks completely surrounded a central space large enough to hold a great number of men. According to legend, its name had come from an Indian tribe that had used it as a temple in which human sacrifices were held. It was an ideal spot for Lafitte's slave auctions. A platform had been erected upon which the Negroes could be exhibited to buyers from New Orleans. Around it the smugglers would group themselves, armed and on guard against any disturbance. In front of the platform New Orleans gentlemen would gather to make their choices of the slaves. Jean Lafitte would wander about among them, chatting agreeably.

There was never anything secret about the auctions, either. Days before one was to take place Lafitte would have his men nail up announcements of it all over New Orleans, advertising slaves and other merchandise for sale at The Temple and inviting all New Orleans to attend. Usually the auctions were well attended. Sometimes as many as a hundred merchants and planters came. Jean Lafitte was getting bolder and bolder. He soon had another place, called Little Temple.

Seldom did anything go wrong at the auctions. The worst that seemed to happen was the coming of one of those quick storms that suddenly sweep the Barataria country. All day there might be nothing but a warm, fragrant breeze. Then, almost in a moment the sky can blacken. A shrieking wind rushes out of the Gulf of Mexico, there is a fearful crashing of thunder, spitting lightning shatters the sky. Trees bend with it and frail houses rock and men flee for their lives. This happened a few times at The Temple and then slaves would escape into the marsh, for not even Lafitte and his men could fight Nature. Often the slaves were rounded up later. If not, the poor creatures were likely to meet a worse end among the slime and the alligators and the deadly moccasins that infested the region.

The citizens of New Orleans seem to have relished the boldness of the Lafittes. They would point them out on the streets with admiration. They mocked the helplessness of the English-speaking authorities they had not yet accepted.

There is a tale of a Sunday afternoon. A large number of Orleanians were strolling in the old square before the St. Louis Cathedral, and most of them were talking about one subject. The night before a young seaman named Williams had arrived in the city to tell a story of horror and bloodshed.

Williams had been one of the crew of the *Independence,* an American merchantman running out of Salem, Massachusetts. The ship was returning from a voyage to the coast of Africa when just out of Havana it had been attacked by pirates. Every member of the crew but Williams had been murdered. He had leaped overboard and had been picked up by another vessel, which had brought him to New Orleans.

The Americans in New Orleans whispered, "Lafitte!" But the other citizens did not believe it. Lafitte, they said, had never been guilty of such a crime. Everyone knew he raided only Spanish ships, and that, according to his letter of marque, he had a right to do so. He had never touched an American vessel.

But a group who were enemies of Jean Lafitte went to call upon Governor Claiborne that Sunday. They found him in conference with the seaman, Williams, and with that same John Randolph Grymes with whom Esau and Mr. Glasscock had visited during their stay in New Orleans. Grymes was now the district attorney.

Later that same afternoon, the crowd near the cathedral were treated to a sight that excited them more than ever. Walking arm in arm, Jean and Pierre Lafitte strolled slowly past, crossed the street and entered the square. There they were for all to see, for the Governor to view if he cared to do so.

People gasped. Those Lafittes! They feared nothing! They were dressed as gentlemen, as if they were on their way to a fashionable dinner. Jean Lafitte paused at a post and read slowly a sign announcing one of his auctions at The Temple. Then the two moved on again, tipping their hats to the ladies. Did they know the gossip that everyone had been discussing? Did they realize they were being accused of piracy and murder?

A man who had more nerve than the rest blocked their path. He addressed Jean Lafitte. "Captain Lafitte," he asked hesitantly, "have you heard of the American ship being attacked?"

Lafitte looked down at the man, for he was

inches taller. His fierce eyes held a flicker of amusement for a moment. "Yes," he said. "I have heard of it."

"The survivor is with the Governor now," the man said, as if to warn Lafitte.

"I hope they catch the scoundrels," said Lafitte.

As the brothers moved away a hum of conversation passed through the crowd. What nerve! What bravery! It was magnificent!

Of course Jean Lafitte had had nothing to do with this terrible act. Yet to appear now, when he and his men were suspected of having committed it, to have appeared deliberately when he knew what was happening—it was incredibly bold!

Suddenly all New Orleans was on the side of the Lafittes and against Williams. Probably the man was not telling the truth, they said. Even if he had been on a ship that was attacked by pirates, why was the ship coming from Africa? It had probably been loaded with slaves, which was illegal anyway. The ship's crew had suffered only what they deserved.

Strangely, John Randolph Grymes seemed to agree. He announced in the newspaper the following day that an American ship carrying an illegal cargo of slaves had been raided by pirates. Nothing more was done about it, and Williams disappeared.

Not even Governor Claiborne seems to have thought the Lafittes guilty of this. But he was worried. He had come to bring law and order to Louisiana, and he was determined something must be done to stop the Lafitte activities. At this very time he was writing to President Madison about the situation, which he said must be handled with calm deliberation and strength. He was entirely conscious of all that was going on down in Barataria, he said, and he was determined to put an end to it. The Lafittes must go.

That week there was another large auction at The Temple.

Beluche · Dominique · Nez Coupé · Gambi

5: Lafitte and His Lieutenants

JEAN LAFITTE SURROUNDED HIMSELF WITH men who were both tough and worthy of his trust. There was Dominique You, the most famous of them all and, after his brother, Pierre, Jean Lafitte's closest friend. There was Beluche, who years later became a commodore in the navy of Venezuela. There was Nez Coupé, so called because he had lost part of his nose in a saber duel, and whose real name was Louis

47

Chighizola. There were Jean Baptiste Sauvinet, who acted as Lafitte's banker, and Thiac the blacksmith. Also there was Gambi, who called himself a pirate openly, and who was the only one to prove troublesome, as we shall see.

It seems to have been Dominique You upon whom Lafitte most depended. In turn Dominique You was completely devoted to Lafitte. You looked like a pirate. Someone has said he resembled "a ruffled eagle." He was short and nearly as broad as his height. He was incredibly strong and he had a raging temper. Yet his outbursts were few and usually he was good-humored and he loved to joke and laugh. It is said even Lafitte would take his teasing.

His life had been filled with adventure and the wildest kind of excitement. He had been born on the island of Santo Domingo in the Caribbean and had run away from home when a young boy to rove the seas on sailing vessels. He had been an artillerist with Napoleon Bonaparte. Later, like Jean Lafitte, he went to Colombia, secured a letter of marque and became a privateer with his own ship and crew, raiding Spanish vessels, seizing their cargoes, and setting them ablaze. Then he heard of

Lafitte and headed for New Orleans to join his forces with those of the greatest privateer of them all.

René Beluche, like Dominique You, had fought in Napoleon's army. Later he had gone to sea, turned privateer, and joined with Lafitte after hearing the stories about him. He commanded another of Lafitte's vessels. Until the end of his life he vowed he had never been a pirate, yet he was fierce-looking and swarthy and inspired fear in most people who met him.

Louis Chighizola, or Nez Coupé, had a face striped with scars, no nose, and had been an old sea dog all his days. Because he settled down on Grand Isle and later in New Orleans where his great-great-great grandchildren still live we know a little more about him than some of the others. His descendants tell many tales of old Nez Coupé and his companions.

One of these stories has to do with a line of live-oak trees that still stand on Grand Isle, and which are supposed to have been planted by Nez Coupé after his privateering days were past. It is said that those trees have protected the island from serious damage for much more than a hundred years. When bad storms come out of the Gulf the trees break the force of the hurricane winds and save the houses and the people. They are a monument to a man called a pirate—a living monument he planted himself.

Another story told by the descendants of Nez Coupé is this tale of the golden thimble:

On a dark midnight the booty of a raided Spanish ship was being divided. Jean and Pierre Lafitte, Dominique You, Beluche and Nez Coupé sat around a center table in Lafitte's house at Grand Terre. Their men packed the room, crowding about to get a look at the riches on the table—silken bags of jewels, heaps of gold coins. Near Jean's feet was a great chest filled with the gold doubloons, which he was measuring out among the men. There was only one woman in the room—Nez Coupé's wife, who stood behind her husband's chair. Everyone was silent and the only sound was the clinking of the coins, for these men took the division of spoils with complete seriousness.

Lafitte was serious about it, too, both serious and fair. There were certain rules. The booty was always divided into parts. A captain received a certain number of parts, the men next in command another number of parts, but fewer than the captain. The lowest ranking seamen received at least one part each. Even the cooks received their division. Of course the largest number of parts went to Jean Lafitte, as leader of the entire gang, as the king.

The dividing went on for hours. Lafitte and his assistants worked tirelessly, and the men came up one by one and carried away their shares. No one seems to have questioned Lafitte's splitting of the spoils. His word was law. Only Gambi, crouched on the floor near the table, looked sullen, but he was always like that and no one paid any attention to him. When his turn came he took what Lafitte meted out to him and left the room. Lafitte shrugged and sighed. That Gambi! He would give him trouble one day.

As dawn brightened the windows the work was done. All the men but the Lafittes and the lieutenants had departed. There was nothing left on the table but two gold doubloons, not yet divided. Lafitte smiled and looked up at the wife of Nez Coupé.

"You take these," he said to her, holding out the coins.

She reached for them, but her husband had

already snatched them from Lafitte's hand. "I will take care of them for her," Nez Coupé said.

Lafitte rose and held out his hand again. "Give them back to me," he said, his eyes blazing at old Nez Coupé.

Nez Coupé returned them reluctantly, and Lafitte gave the coins to Dominique You. "Take these to old Thiac the blacksmith," he said, "and have a gold thimble made for madame."

Dominque You laughed heartily. He thought it was a fine joke on Nez Coupé, who was always greedy.

That gold thimble is still in the family of Nez Coupé who live on Grand Isle.

Like the brothers Lafitte, the lieutenants were often seen in New Orleans. Unlike the Lafittes, they were not always popular. They looked like pirates and most of the time they acted like them. Now and then there were lively incidents.

It took New Orleans a long time to forget the evening when Lafitte and his lieutenants went to General Humbert's birthday dinner.

General Humbert was a hero of Napoleon's army, an old soldier who had fought both in

Europe and in Santo Domingo. After a quarrel with Napoleon, Humbert was exiled and came to New Orleans to retire. In 1812 a group of his friends gave him a birthday dinner at a place called the Hôtel de la Marine. Around the table, among others, were Jean and Pierre Lafitte, Dominique You, Beluche, Nez Coupé, Gambi, Sauvinet, and Thiac. They all toasted Jean Robert Marie Humbert's fifty-seventh birthday, and he toasted them in return. There was wonderful food, crab gumbo, roast turkey, and lots of other things.

At the end of the dinner one man rose and made a speech, telling of General Humbert's heroic deeds. Suddenly the general's face began to redden, and before anyone realized what was happening he sprang to his feet and began shouting, "What am I doing here among pirates and outlaws? Why are these men here?"

Lafitte's men glowered.

"Pirates!" General Humbert shouted again. "Cutthroats!"

One of the men who was not with the Lafitte party tried to quiet the general, but he bellowed, "I will have my say! I will not remain here with outlaws and murderers!"

There was a threatening silence and then Lafitte's men rose. Daggers shone in the candlelight. "You will not say that again!" said Beluche, his swarthy face even darker than usual.

"You are a murderer!" cried Humbert again. "A murderer, a pirate, and a thief!"

"I kill!" shouted Beluche and would have sprung upon the old man. But Jean Lafitte had risen and was between them.

"Be quiet," he ordered Beluche.

Then the old soldier stumbled forward and fell upon Lafitte's shoulder and burst into tears.

"It is all right," said Lafitte. "It is over." But his dark eyes still smoldered.

"I did not mean you," General Humbert muttered. "You know I did not mean you!"

Lafitte was silent as the general was led out of the room. A few moments later he and his men left. What must have worried him most was that the next day everyone in New Orleans would hear about it. No matter what the general had said at the end he, Jean Lafitte, had been called a cutthroat, a murderer and a pirate.

6: Mutiny at Barataria

It was about the time of General Humbert's dinner that trouble began to come to Jean Lafitte. Not that he was any less bold or any less brave. He went on doing all the things he had always done. He was seen in New Orleans as often as usual. He still had the signs put up announcing the auctions at The Temple. He still ruled his islands and the swampland with as strong a hand and will as ever. But he felt that his enemies were increasing in number.

Even in New Orleans the group that was against him was growing. Many terrible tales came from the Gulf of Mexico and the Caribbean Sea. Piracy was on the increase. Ships of all nations were being attacked. Sometimes survivors came to New Orleans with their gruesome stories. At other times ships vanished completely in perfect, calm weather. The stories came not only from visitors to New Orleans, but also from Havana, then from New York, Salem, Boston, Philadelphia, and Charleston. The citizens of New Orleans began to complain that they were afraid to leave the city by ship and start a journey to any of those places. They were afraid to send their children to France for their schooling, as had long been their custom. More and more these happenings and these fears were blamed upon Jean Lafitte.

Whenever Lafitte had a chance to do so he denied all charges of piracy, as he had always done. Half the tales told were not true, he said. As to those that were, he had no knowledge of whatever it was that had taken place.

As further proof of his innocence, perhaps, he was soon being seen about even more than before. He seems always to have chosen a time when there would be the greatest number of people on the streets to come strolling along, bowing to friends, stopping to chat. He began appearing at country balls, talking to planters and merchants, and inviting them to Grande Terre, to Grand Isle, to the auctions at The Temple. Often high-spirited country youths and planters' sons in search of adventure, came to Barataria and joined his band. By this time he had more than a thousand men working with him and at least a dozen ships.

Yet the signs of warning continued to become more numerous. Governor Claiborne was determined to break the power of Jean Lafitte. He held conferences with other officials, sent constant dispatches to Washington which asked for aid against "these smugglers and pirates." He met, too, with customs officials, who were complaining that the smugglers were ruining the city's commerce, that ships of the United States had been attacked. Yet they could collect proof of nothing. None of Lafitte's men had ever been captured in the act of committing a crime. New Orleans was still too small to have a large enough police force or militia to invade Lafitte's kingdom. Until now at least it was thought that such an attempt would be too dangerous. The men who might be used for that purpose did not know the swamps. Anything might happen to them.

But the government officials and the growing fear of the people were only part of Jean Lafitte's troubles. He had at least one outbreak at Grand Terre, this time within his own group of men.

Gambi had always been the least trustworthy of his lieutenants. The man was brave, but he was disagreeable and evil. He preferred to call himself a pirate and to strut about boasting of his wicked past. He was a small but wiry man, burned black by the sun, who wore ferocious mustaches, a kerchief around his head, an earring in one ear, and a pistol on each hip.

Lafitte let Gambi boast and talk, but he watched him closely. Then one day Gambi came back to Grande Terre and announced that his ship had attacked and sunk an American merchantman in the Gulf of Mexico.

This was against Lafitte's strictest orders. He had never wanted an American ship harmed by his men. He summoned his lieutenants together for a meeting. They grouped around Gambi—Pierre Lafitte, Dominique You, Bel-

uche, Nez Coupé and several others. The charge
Lafitte brought against Gambi was of being
guilty of the crime he hated—piracy.

"This can ruin us all," Lafitte said. "You
have given the American authorities a chance
to charge us all with piracy. They have been
waiting for this for a long time."

"They will never know it," said Gambi,
bristling.

"We can't be sure of that," said Lafitte. "It
must never happen again."

At this Gambi flew into a rage. He refused
to promise not to attack American ships again.
"I am a pirate," he said. "We are all pirates!
Why be a liar and a hypocrite?"

Lafitte bounded away from the table and
leaped at Gambi, but Nez Coupé separated
them. "Let him go now if he wants to go. Gambi
was here before any of us," he said.

It was true. Gambi had been operating out
of Grande Terre before Lafitte had arrived in
the country. Perhaps it was jealousy of his
leadership that had made Gambi as he was.

"Get out!" shouted Lafitte to Gambi. Then,
"Are you willing to follow my orders?" he asked
Nez Coupé.

"I am."

Lafitte looked around the room. "No American vessel is ever to be touched by any of my men," he said. "Is that understood?"

They all nodded. Gambi, who had paused at the door, went out into the hot sun, his men following him.

But it was not over. A few hours later a group of Gambi's men gathered outside Lafitte's own house, muttering and whispering among themselves. Gambi was nowhere in sight. Lafitte, peering through his barred windows, knew that this was mutiny.

As usual he decided upon the boldest course of action as being the best. He flung open his door and stepped out onto the wide veranda, a pistol in his hand.

The men shouted at him. Gambi should be the leader, they said. They would take orders from no one but him. He had been there the longest and so he should rule. They were tired of Lafitte's laws. They wanted to attack any ship they pleased.

A tall young man stepped out in front of the others.

"Gambi is our leader!" he said. "We will take

orders from him, not from Lafitte." He raised the pistol in his hand.

Lafitte fired first, for no man in his band was quicker with a trigger. Before the smoke had vanished from the barrel of his pistol Gambi's men were carrying away the dead body of the defiant mutineer. After that there was silence.

Lafitte had won again.

7: *The Arrest of Jean Lafitte*

I N 1812 THE UNITED STATES WAS AT WAR WITH
England for the second time. This struggle was
to change Jean Lafitte's whole life, although
he did not know it yet.

But Governor Claiborne soon realized that
the war made the Lafitte corsairs even more
dangerous than before. The Governor became
more and more worried. There were the Lafittes,
he reflected, in complete control of all the land

at the mouth of the Mississippi River. If the British were to try to invade New Orleans that was the way they would come. The Governor had reason to fear that the privateers—he called them pirates—might aid the British. These pirates must go, he told the men around him. It would not be easy.

It is hard to believe now, but we must remember that at the outbreak of the War of 1812 the United States had an army of less than 6,000 men. Jean Lafitte had 1,000 men under his own control. Congress increased the army to 25,000 after war was declared, but there were still no men to spare. As a result, Claiborne could expect no aid from the Government in Washington against the Baratarians.

A year before there had been an uprising of slaves about thirty-five miles from New Orleans. After the revolt had been put down blame had been placed on the wild Africans lately brought into Louisiana by the Lafittes. At that time Claiborne had asked the Legislature of Louisiana for a militia to send against the Baratarians. It was refused. He was told it would cost too much.

Now, in 1812, Governor Claiborne tried a new

method. He appealed to the customs officials, who had long been enraged by the smuggling. At last he got some action. A kind of coast guard consisting of forty dragoons and a few small boats was formed under the command of Captain Andrew Hunter Holmes. Captain Holmes was not expected to arrest all the Baratarians with this small number of men. He had one principal order: "Get the brothers Lafitte!"

Lafitte roared with laughter when he heard of Holmes and his dragoons daring to hope to capture him.

As they sailed their boats through the bayous, Holmes and his men questioned fishermen and trappers and the news reached Lafitte at once. He had no fear that the dragoons would attempt to attack Grande Terre. Nevertheless, he ordered his men to strengthen the crude fort he had erected there long before. When this was done he had cannon set up, and the guard along the beaches was doubled. Now let them come!

"We'll take them all prisoner," said Dominique You, "and send them back to Claiborne with signs on their backs."

Yet Lafitte was too intelligent to make a joke of it entirely. He and Pierre began leading the expeditions to the city themselves, taking devious routes far from where they knew Holmes was camping. For weeks contraband continued to move into New Orleans, increasing Claiborne's fury.

Meanwhile the war with England went on. The Americans, under General William Hull, attacked Canada, but this resulted in failure. General Hull was forced to surrender Detroit to the British.

The New York militia refused to follow their commander, General Stephen Van Rensselaer, across the frontier at Niagara. An attempt to invade Montreal also failed.

The British talked of invading various parts of the United States, including New Orleans. They would sail up the Mississippi River from the Gulf of Mexico, they boasted, and conquer all the Mississippi Valley.

Claiborne felt that the British might find this an easy task as long as the Lafittes ruled the mouth of the river.

Meanwhile, Captain Holmes bided his time

and waited. His expedition of forty dragoons had set out early in the spring. Summer came and then the autumn. All this time the Lafittes eluded him. Holmes' men grew tired and discouraged. Their camps were terribly uncomfortable. There was plenty of food to be had, but the mosquitoes nearly drove them mad. The weather was first beastly hot, then wet and cold. Holmes must have heard the mocking laughter of the Baratarians grow louder and louder in his ears.

Then it happened, quite suddenly. On the night of November 16 Holmes and his men came almost by accident to the bank of a bayou. There, loading a half dozen pirogues—which are small, slender skiffs still used in Louisiana— were Jean and Pierre Lafitte and some twenty- five men. Patience had rewarded Holmes. The smugglers were armed, but they were hopelessly outnumbered. Jean Lafitte greeted Holmes politely and surrendered his men. All of them and the loot with which the pirogues were loaded were taken back to New Orleans at once. Only one smuggler ran away and he was shot dead.

For the first time in his life Jean Lafitte was under arrest. Yet he was in good spirits even after the jailer turned the key in the lock of his cell at the old Cabildo. He knew he would not stay in jail long.

8: Lafitte the Outlaw

HE DID NOT REMAIN IN JAIL LONG. THE NEXT day his banker, Jean Baptiste Sauvinet, appeared, put up the necessary bond money, and Jean, Pierre and their men were released at once. That very afternoon the Lafittes strolled jauntily through New Orleans for all to see. Their admirers again stared at them with awe, and especially at Jean Lafitte. What a man!

Their trial came up about two weeks later, on November 29. Neither of the Lafittes appeared in court. They were, instead, represented by Sauvinet. Captain Holmes appeared and told the detailed story of the capture. Charges of smuggling were placed against each man, but what could be done? All of them had again vanished into the Baratarian swamps. Unless they appeared of their own free will it meant that they would have to be caught all over again. They did not appear of their own free will. All the work that Captain Holmes had done was useless.

The case came up again in April 1813, again in July, and once more in October. Neither of the Lafittes nor any of their men made an appearance. Finally John Randolph Grymes, as district attorney, won a judgment of $1214.52 for the Government. This was for the contraband in the pirogues when Holmes had taken his prisoners. The banker Sauvinet paid this gladly. That small amount of money was nothing compared to the wealth of the Lafittes.

Yet, although he was free, this judgment changed everything for Jean Lafitte. For the first time he had been convicted of smuggling in a court of law. Until now Claiborne might privately call him a pirate, might even do so before other city and Government officials, but he had had no proof against him. Now it was different. The merchandise Holmes had seized had been proved smuggled goods. Now Lafitte was a fugitive, an outlaw, subject to arrest at any time he could be caught.

Despite this, the Lafittes had never had such a profitable year as 1813. With the war in progress people wanted Lafitte's goods more than ever. To supply the demand his ships plowed the Gulf of Mexico and the Caribbean Sea more boldly than before, defying all nations, even the British vessels which were beginning to appear in those waters.

Neither did the judgment keep the Baratarians out of New Orleans. Some of them were always about, swaggering and blustering and squandering their money. They adroitly avoided arrest by the city guards, and engaged in free-for-all fights with Mississippi flatboatmen, who had come down the river to New Orleans with their flatboats of merchandise. These men were admitted to be every bit as tough as were the Baratarians.

Even Jean and Pierre Lafitte still came to New Orleans, but more cautiously now. They spent their time among friends and avoided crowds in which there might be men who would report their presence to Claiborne.

Gradually all the crimes that took place in New Orleans began to be blamed upon the Baratarians. They were charged with being thieves and thugs, with setting fire to buildings, with committing murder in the streets.

Claiborne continued to worry about Lafitte and his men, but he was now even more worried about the war. A thousand rumors of the British preparations to invade New Orleans reached him. He knew that elsewhere the war news was bad. Detroit had been in British hands since the year before. The *Constitution* had sunk the British *Guerrière*, but the United States *Chesapeake* had been captured by the English *Shannon*. It was already being whispered that the Federal authorities might have to flee Washington.

Besides all this, there were Indian troubles, partially, perhaps, set in motion by the British. Close to New Orleans, Fort Sims at Mobile had been attacked by the Creeks and more than 350 men, women and children had been slaughtered. Joining the Indians were fugitive slaves who aided the Indians in the massacre. Claiborne feared that the Choctaws near New Orleans might be stirred to similar violence. The situation was terrifying and Claiborne did everything he could, but it was almost too much for one man. He could not give much time to pursuing the Baratarian smugglers.

At about the same time Jean Lafitte had his own private war with the British. For some time British merchantmen had been raided and they were tired of it. In June 1813 a British sloop anchored near Grand Isle and sent in a boatload of marines in an attempt to clean out Lafitte's band. The marines approached two of Lafitte's ships and began an attack.

But the British had known nothing of the strength of the Baratarians. They soon retreated with heavy losses, reboarded their sloop, hauled anchor, and sailed away in a hurry. They never again attempted to fight the Baratarians in this way.

Claiborne then made one more attempt to stop the operations of Lafitte. He learned that the Baratarians, becoming bolder, were now bringing their swift ships up the bayous to plantations only a few miles from New Orleans.

Some of the ships had been seen at Donaldson-ville, on the other side of the river not far from the city. Furthermore he learned that the auctions at The Temple were not only still going on, but that they were larger than ever and that they were attended by more people than ever. Indeed, he was told that some of his closest friends went regularly to The Temple. Often he himself saw announcements of the auctions. During the night these had been nailed on lamp posts along the streets.

So Governor Claiborne issued a public proclamation, stating that the Lafittes and their Baratarians were outlaws and criminals. It called upon all citizens to aid him in catching the leaders and he made it a crime to have anything to do with the Lafittes or to buy anything from them. The proclamation was clearly a charge against the Lafittes but their names were never mentioned. Claiborne referred to them as "a considerable Banditti . . . . upon or near the shores of Lake Barataria," and he spoke of their "ill begotten treasure" of which "no Man can partake, without being forever dishonored, and exposing himself to the severest punishment."

Now the citizens of New Orleans were subject to arrest if they did business with the Lafittes!

When Jean Lafitte read it he laughed, but his eyes were angry. It was no worse than before, he said. People would pay no attention to it. "I would as soon drown in ten feet of water as six!" he said.

The next afternoon he walked into a New Orleans coffee house and denounced Claiborne to the gentlemen gathered there. This man Claiborne was a coward, he said. Why had he not dared to call him by his name? His name was Jean Lafitte! Neither he nor his men were banditti! They were no more bandits than they were pirates. They were privateersmen, perhaps smugglers, but not bandits. That was a lie! Why did not Claiborne come and arrest him now?

He did not care, he said. He had been at war with Spain all his life. Lately he had been at war with England. Now the United States had declared him an enemy. Let Claiborne catch him if he could!

Then he stalked out and left them all staring after him.

9: A Price on His Head

WHEN LAFITTE SAID THE UNITED STATES
had declared him an enemy he meant Governor
Claiborne. Lafitte never considered himself an
enemy of America. By now he felt he was an
American. He never allowed his men to attack
an American ship or to harm a citizen of the
United States. He had risked mutiny to make
sure that Gambi never raided a United States
vessel again. Lafitte loved freedom more than

75

anything in the world, and the United States was a free country. Even his beloved France was under the heel of a tyrant: Napoleon. So his affection went to America.

On several occasions Lafitte went out of his way to help Americans. One day a Louisiana planter, a Mr. Martin, and several friends were caught in a storm in the Gulf of Mexico aboard a small private boat belonging to Mr. Martin. Several of the men were swept overboard and the boat was already half sunk when one of Lafitte's ships reached it. The survivors were carried ashore and brought to Grande Terre, to the house of Jean Lafitte.

As Mr. Martin told the story later, Lafitte seemed to him the kindest of men. The survivors were fed and given new clothes. A privateer who knew something of medicine treated several who were injured. When all were able to travel again Lafitte placed a schooner at their disposal and stocked it with all sorts of provisions.

Mrs. Martin, writing later about this incident in a letter to a friend, said that Lafitte gave her husband everything he had lost in the storm. Then Lafitte asked him if he had a family. Mr.

Martin said he did. Lafitte added a keg of rare wine and a pineapple cheese as presents for Mrs. Martin. The memory the Martins always had of Jean Lafitte was a fine one.

This had all taken place in 1812. Mr. Martin did not meet Lafitte again until more than a year later. The second meeting took place in a little inn near Berwick Bay. One day Mr. and Mrs. Martin were on their way by carriage to visit Mrs. Martin's father in Nashville, Tennessee. They stayed overnight at the inn and the next morning when they came downstairs for break-fast a servant told Mr. Martin a gentleman wished to see him in a private room. Mr. Martin followed the servant. When he entered the room there stood Jean Lafitte. Lafitte looked fine, and he was as bold as ever. Yet he was in hiding now.

"Sir, I can trust you?" Lafitte asked.

"You can," said Mr. Martin. "I'll never for-get your kindness to me and whatever I can do for you will be done with pleasure."

Lafitte handed Mr. Martin a packet of letters. "You will deliver these letters to such gentle-men as I direct, living in Donaldsonville," he said. "Sir, when I learned you were here this morning I decided to put these letters in your charge. I feel that they will be safely delivered."

Mr. Martin never told any more about the letters or to whom he did deliver them. But they must have been addressed to men in Donaldsonville with whom Lafitte had business. In that way Mr. Martin repaid his debt.

In October 1813 Governor Claiborne made another attempt to capture Lafitte. This time, he vowed, if he had Lafitte in jail again he would not be released on bail. He would remain in jail, go on trail, and be sentenced.

Lafitte knew this and he became more and more cautious. He was sometimes seen in New Orleans, but very seldom. He spent nearly all his time at Grande Terre. When business forced him to appear elsewhere it was at night and in secret, or in some out-of-the-way place such as the inn at Berwick Bay where he had met Mr. Martin. He became angrier all the time. He hated having to hide.

Several times he was almost caught. On October 14, 1813 a company of dragoons, led by a revenue officer named Walter Gilbert, surprised Lafitte and some of his men in the swamps not far from The Temple. This time the Baratarians did not surrender as they had to Captain Holmes. There was a skirmish and Lafitte and his men drove off the soldiers and escaped into the marshes.

On another occasion Lafitte had a dangerous but amusing adventure with Mrs. Claiborne, none other than the Governor's own wife. Lafitte was visiting with some friends on a great plantation not far from New Orleans, a place where he often stopped to spend the night when he was traveling through the country. Lafitte and the planter's family had just finished supper when a servant came into the dining room and announced that Mrs. Claiborne had come to call. There was much excitement, but there was not even time to hide Lafitte. Mrs. Claiborne walked right into the room!

The planter's wife thought quickly. She introduced Lafitte as "Mr. Clement," then rushed out to warn the servants. Everybody played his part well and Mrs. Claiborne had no idea until months later as to the identity of the polite and handsome young man who was so gallant and who kept her laughing all evening. Both Lafitte and Mrs. Claiborne stayed overnight, of course,

for people always did in the Louisiana planta·
tion country in those days. In the morning they
had breakfast together and then Lafitte escorted
the Governor's wife to her carriage. Afterwards
Mrs. Claiborne told everyone how much she
admired "Mr. Clement." She was to know who
Jean Lafitte was the next time they met, but
we'll learn about that later. For the moment
Lafitte felt it was a good joke on Claiborne.

But Governor Claiborne was not joking now
at all. He made one more appeal to the State
Legislature for men and money to attack the
strongholds of the Baratarians with force. This
was refused. Neither men nor money could be
spared.

Then he issued another proclamation. This
time he named Jean Lafitte. The Governor
charged that Lafitte and his men had attacked
Walter Gilbert and the dragoons and that one
of the soldiers had been wounded in the fight.
He said that Lafitte had terrorized the people
of the State for some time. He offered five
hundred dollars reward for the capture of Jean
Lafitte and for his delivery to the sheriff of New
Orleans or to any sheriff in the State of

Louisiana. It was rumored that he planned to put Jean Lafitte to death.

This was on November 24, 1813. Lafitte took another chance at showing the people of New Orleans how bold he was. The next day he strolled through New Orleans, stopping to read the proclamation, copies of which the Governor had had nailed up on the lampposts and in all public places. No one touched Lafitte and the people in the streets grinned when they saw him.

The following day people were even more astonished. All the proclamations of Governor Claiborne had vanished during the night. In their places were copies of another one. This proclamation offered $1500 reward—three times the amount the Governor had offered—to anyone who would capture William C. C. Claiborne, Governor of Louisiana, and deliver him to Jean Lafitte at Grande Terre. It was, of course, signed "Jean Lafitte."

It was the most daring stunt of Lafitte's career! Everyone laughed but Governor Claiborne.

10: Pierre in the Calaboose

GOVERNOR CLAIBORNE WAS AN INTELLI
gent man. Also, in his own way, he was a
brave as Jean Lafitte. He was trying to do the
best job he could, and as he saw it he could
not allow the Lafittes to continue their smuggling
or their defiance of his authority. He had been
sent down to New Orleans to keep law and
order. What he feared most perhaps was that
the Baratarians would join with the British in
attacking New Orleans, or that they would at
least help the British to invade the city.

Claiborne had no idea of Jean Lafitte's sympathies in the war going on. Perhaps if the two men could have met and talked they might have understood each other better. That is usually true, but men seldom act that way. Claiborne continued to fight Lafitte as best he could, and Lafitte fought back.

To Claiborne Lafitte was a pirate, a Frenchman by blood. Moreover, England and France were now friends. How could Claiborne be sure Lafitte did not favor the British? With British warships out there in the Gulf, just a few miles from New Orleans, the Governor felt the city was in grave danger. He knew that sooner or later there would be fighting for the city. England had announced that she would capture New Orleans and that she would give Louisiana back to Spain. It was a terrible thought and it worried Claiborne constantly.

The war was not going well in other parts of the country, either, and Claiborne knew that New Orleans would have to fight it out almost alone. Few troops could be spared to this part of the country that was so far from New York and Washington.

So one of the first things Claiborne hoped to do was to end the Baratarians' control of the swamps below the city and the Gulf. With them gone, he felt at least one danger would be past. The best way to do this, he knew, was to capture the leader, Jean Lafitte. Without a leader, the privateers might not stand together.

In December, a month after the appearance of the proclamation offering a reward for Lafitte —and Lafitte's proclamation offering a reward for Claiborne—General Flournoy, in charge of the United States forces on the Mississippi, wrote to Claiborne. The General said that he could not offer Louisiana more than 700 men to help defend New Orleans from the British.

This was a dark hour for Claiborne. Not only could he expect no help against the Baratarians, but he could hardly expect any in defending the city against the British.

Then there came a little good news. General Andrew Jackson of Tennessee had won the war with the Indians near Mobile. Claiborne began to hope that Jackson and his men might reach New Orleans in time. Jackson was the toughest fighting man in the country. With his aid there might be a chance.

In January handbills appeared all over New Orleans announcing another auction at The

Temple. They appeared, as usual, during the night and they were signed by Jean Lafitte. Claiborne ground his teeth with rage. He went into conference with the United States Collector of Customs. The Collector did what he could, which was very little. He sent a group of twelve under a man named Stout with orders to prevent the Lafittes and the Baratarians from using The Temple as an auction place. It was a puny and tragic attempt.

A few days later news of what had happened reached the city. The Collector's men had fought it out with the Baratarians. Stout was dead and all the other men were prisoners of the privateers. Another appeal was made to the State. This time some militia were organized. They vanished into the swamps and Claiborne waited.

When they reappeared the Governor was in a worse position than ever. Lafitte had captured the entire militia, then released them and sent them back to the city, not only unharmed, but loaded with expensive gifts! Some of the men went about saying what a fine fellow this Lafitte was!

Claiborne must have wondered if anybody wanted to fight Lafitte except himself. Indeed, not many did. To most people he was already a hero, a kind of Robin Hood. To the Governor it was embarrassing and infuriating. A New Orleans newspaper, printed in French, was openly making fun of him. He could hear the whole city laughing.

But he would not give up, so he tried one more thing. Calling a meeting of the leading businessmen and bankers, Claiborne selected a Grand Jury. Before this Grand Jury he summoned witnesses who knew something about the Baratarians—or said they did. These men swore that they knew Lafitte and his privateers to be guilty of piracy. We do not know how many told the truth, but at the end of it charges of piracy were placed against Jean and Pierre Lafitte, Belouche and Dominique You. It was a serious charge, punishable by death. Before only Jean had been threatened. Now all were condemned.

At this time, while the Grand Jury was meeting, Claiborne had his first stroke of luck so far as the Lafittes were concerned. One afternoon Pierre Lafitte went strolling through New Orleans, perhaps in another act of outright defiance. He spoke to friends as he walked along, and the gossip that he was in New Orleans spread quickly through the city. Everyone knew what Claiborne was doing now, even though the investigation was being held in secret. Pierre Lafitte knew it, too, they said. Like his brother he was showing the Governor that he did not fear him.

But near the St. Louis Cathedral a platoon of soldiers appeared, surrounded Pierre, and placed him under arrest. Someone must have notified Claiborne he was in the city, or else he had simply been recognized by the soldiers. He was taken to the old calaboose—or jail—in the Cabildo, where Claiborne had his official offices, and put in chains in a cell.

Jean came to New Orleans at once and his banker, Sauvinet, tried to bail Pierre out. This time bail was denied. So far as Claiborne was concerned, Pierre would rot in jail. The Governor knew that once released the bail would mean nothing. The Lafittes could well afford to lose the money and Pierre would run off into the swamps again, as Jean Lafitte had done when he had been arrested some time ago.

Jean Lafitte went back to Barataria without his brother, coming into and leaving the city in secret this time, careful to avoid arrest. If he were caught there would be no hope of getting Pierre out. But Jean was not discouraged. He knew he would think of something. He always thought he could outwit Claiborne.

But Claiborne's triumph in having Pierre Lafitte in chains was overshadowed by many other things, most of them related to the war. As the summer of 1814 approached, the war news seemed to grow worse every day. At that time it took a long while for news to arrive from other parts of the country. We must remember this was long before the telegraph or any of the other means by which we can now know almost immediately what is going on all over the world. Letters and dispatches from the eastern coast of the United States, from New York and Washington had to travel part of the way by a carrier on horseback. Often, too, they were carried by river boats down the Mississippi to New Orleans. It took weeks and months.

In August New Orleans learned that the British had landed near Washington and set fire to the Capitol. President Madison and his cabinet had been forced to flee the city. Dolly Madison had followed, carrying with her the Declaration of Independence. A prisoner aboard an English ship at Baltimore, Francis Scott Key, watched the bombing of Fort Henry and began writing "The Star Spangled Banner."

News of the burning of Washington stunned the people of New Orleans, especially those like Claiborne who were American born. It seemed to justify everything the Governor had said and everything he had feared. The British might win this war. If they did, the American Revolution might have been fought for nothing. It would be the end of this great, growing new nation and all the dreams of the men who had made it free. We can imagine how we would feel today if Washington were set on fire by an enemy.

But there was no panic anywhere. America went on fighting. As in every other part of the nation, people in New Orleans prepared to fight as best they could. Governor Claiborne kept asking the Federal authorities for help, both against the British and the Baratarians. His hope of aid from General Jackson faded a little, for there was no further news from him or of his coming to the city. New Orleans braced itself to fight its battle alone.

In the meantime Pierre Lafitte remained in jail. All through the spring and summer months he sat in the tiny cell, which you can see to this day in the Cabildo in New Orleans. Heavy chains about his ankles and arms allowed him to walk no more than part way across the small space of the cell. His food was coarse. He was dirty and hot and miserable.

During the summer Pierre became ill and he asked that the chains be removed. Governor Claiborne sent two doctors to examine him. They reported that the chains were not making Pierre sick. It was his state of mind, they said. This was probably true. No Lafitte was born to live in chains. The chains remained, however. Claiborne was taking no chances. Pierre might escape.

Now and then Pierre did get news from his brother. The business at Barataria continued to thrive, although the privateers had to be much more cautious than before. Jean Lafitte had hired the best lawyers in the city to help get Pierre out of the calaboose. It would take time, however, Jean said in his messages. Pierre was to be patient. But Pierre grew worse and worse. Sometimes he ran a high fever and was delirious.

Yet he was interested in the war news, when his jailers would tell him about what was going on. Now and then one of his jailers would taunt him by telling him that *if* the British conquered the city maybe they would set him free. They would repeat rumors that Jean Lafitte was plotting with the British against Claiborne and the American Government. Such rumors did exist.

This always sent Pierre Lafitte into a rage.

"We are not with the English!" he would cry. "We have never been with the English. Many of our Baratarians are Americans. We are for Louisiana and the United States!"

No one believed him then.

11: Lafitte and Mr. Grymes

JOHN RANDOLPH GRYMES, THE FRIEND OF ESAU Glasscock and his father and now the district attorney, was the lawyer to whom Jean Lafitte went for help in getting Pierre out of the calaboose.

This was a strange and surprising thing. As district attorney, Mr. Grymes was supposed to be the man who would try to convict Pierre when he came to trial. Ordinarily, you cannot expect the district attorney to defend you or to get you out of jail.

But Grymes was a surprising man. He was one of the most interesting men who ever lived in New Orleans. For many years he had been a friend of Jean Lafitte's. He had even been a guest of Pierre and Jean at Grande Terre on a number of occasions. It was known in the city that Grymes did not agree with Governor Claiborne about the Baratarians. So perhaps he was not entirely surprised when Jean Lafitte asked to see him.

Since Jean could not appear openly in the city, the meeting had to be carefully arranged. A messenger was sent for Grymes and he was taken to a small cottage one night where Jean Lafitte awaited him. Lafitte stated his business at once. He wanted Grymes and his law partner, Edward Livingston, to defend Pierre and any other Baratarians who might get into trouble. As usual Lafitte had acted with directness and boldness. There were no finer lawyers in the nation than Grymes and Livingston, and Lafitte knew this. He wanted the best. Grymes was brilliant and a powerful man in the city. Edward Livingston was a lawyer of great reputation, a brother of the Robert Livingston who had been a major figure in the drafting of the Declaration of Independence. Robert Livingston had also been a friend of George Washington's. Edward Livingston's career had been nearly as distinguished as that of his brother. Grymes and Livingston were important men. They were also intimate friends of Claiborne's.

Of course we can't know what Lafitte and Grymes said to each other in that cottage that night, but we do know that they talked for more than an hour. When the talk was over Grymes and Livingston were attorneys for the Lafittes.

The next day it was announced that John Randolph Grymes had resigned as district attorney. The Lafittes had engaged him and his partner. New Orleans rocked with the news. Those Lafittes! They could even snatch the district attorney from under the Governor's nose!

Grymes and Livingston had been paid twenty thousand dollars each as a fee, a huge sum in those days. Yet it could not have been money that made Grymes resign as district attorney and take the Lafitte case. Grymes was a very rich man. Many New Orleans citizens felt that if Grymes and Livingston were willing to defend the Lafittes, then the two brothers could not be criminals.

But even these men could not get Pierre Lafitte out of the calaboose. They went to court, but it did not help Pierre. He remained in jail. During the trial the new district attorney told Grymes he had lost his honor and had sold out for "the blood-stained gold of pirates." Grymes challenged him to a duel. When they met at dawn a few mornings later Grymes shot him through the hip and left him a cripple for life.

Grymes went on working for Pierre. Then he and Livingston tried to have the prisoner's chains removed. Again Claiborne refused. Not even his friendship for Grymes could make the Governor relent.

Now Grymes spent a lot of time with Jean Lafitte at Grande Terre. When he was in New Orleans he spoke well of Lafitte to his friends If Lafitte were a pirate, he said, then he did not know what a pirate was. He even began to say that Lafitte wanted friendship with Claiborne, and that Lafitte was more interested in the safety and protection of Louisiana than anything else. Naturally Lafitte was bitter, especially about the charges Claiborne had placed against him and about Pierre's being kept in jail, but he was on America's side, Grymes insisted.

Claiborne now made other charges. He announced that Beluche, in command of a privateer vessel, had raided the *Santa,* a Spanish ship, and seized nine thousand dollars in gold from the boat. He also declared that Dominique You and the crew of his ship had captured another Spanish ship near Trinidad and made off with thirty thousand dollars in doubloons. Pierre Lafitte was charged as being an accessory in both cases.

Grymes and Livingston assured Lafitte that these acts could not be proven against Pierre. He might be convicted of privateering, but never of piracy. He had never attacked an American vessel. Furthermore, Claiborne had no authority to place charges about Spanish ships.

Then, as usual in the case of the Lafittes, the unexpected happened. Pierre Lafitte escaped!

How he escaped must remain one of the mysteries concerning the Lafittes. He was in heavy chains, which were attached to a brick wall. He was allowed just enough movement to sit and lie down at night. There were jailers outside his barred cell door. He was, we are told, ill and weak, for he had been in the calaboose for months. Yet one morning he was gone. The chains had been cut and hung loosely from their hooks in the wall.

We can use our imaginations and guess what happened. The Lafittes had many friends. Jean Lafitte was determined his brother would not remain in chains forever. They also had money and possibly the jailers could be bribed. Jean Lafitte, always daring, may have led a group of men to the jail himself the night Pierre escaped. He may have talked to the jailers and pressed gold into their hands. In those days most jailers were rough and not too honest. Or perhaps Jean did not come himself, but sent others. Whatever happened there was no fighting, no excitement that night. In the morning a jailer told the authorities that Pierre Lafitte had vanished during the night. That was all. Three Negro prisoners also escaped.

A notice which is still preserved in a New Orleans museum and in the libraries appeared in the newspapers the next day. It reads:

$1000 REWARD

Will be paid for the apprehension of *Pierre Lafitte,* who broke out and escaped last night from the prison of the parish. Said *Pierre Lafitte* is about five feet ten inches in height, stout made, light complexion, and somewhat crosseyed; further description is unnecessary, as he is very well known in the city.

Said *Lafitte* took with him three negroes. The above reward will be paid to any person delivering the said *Lafitte* to the subscriber.

J. H. Holland,
Keeper of the Prison.

No one else seems to have said anything. Claiborne was silent, at least for the moment. Most people in New Orleans were not surprised. They were astonished that Pierre had remained in jail so long. It was now September. He had been locked up since spring.

When he reached Grande Terre Pierre found much excitement about another matter. He seems to have recovered from his illness at once and to have joined Jean Lafitte in arriving at the decisions that now had to be made. These decisions were the most important they had ever had to make. They were to change their whole lives.

12: The British Bribe

JUST A SHORT TIME BEFORE PIERRE HAD ESCAPED from jail British officers and men had held a meeting with Jean Lafitte. The British had considered this idea a long time. It seemed to them that Lafitte might help them. A buccaneer could be bought.

Their thinking was natural enough. To these dignified English gentlemen, as to Claiborne, Lafitte was an outlaw and a criminal who could be paid to do anything. Besides, the British argued among themselves, Lafitte had no reason to love the American authorities. So they made an appointment by messenger, strapped on their shining swords, and went to meet the leader of the Baratarians.

They approached Grande Terre on the third of September and announced themselves in the proper manner, with the firing of a cannon. Lafitte's men swarmed to the beach to see the brig-of-war, with England's flag rippling in the breeze. When a small boat left the ship, Lafitte set out to meet it in a boat of his own. He invited the two naval officers and the army officer to proceed with him to his island. One of the naval officers identified himself as Captain Lockyer, introduced his lieutenant, and then the scarlet-clad army officer, who was a Captain McWilliams. Lafitte insisted they join him at breakfast.

The British were impressed with what followed. The breakfast lasted for hours. Jean Lafitte was even more elegant than usual. Like everyone else who met him, these stiff and formal Englishmen found it hard to believe that this was the Lafitte they had heard so much about. He was an educated man, they discovered. His manners matched their own. His table was set with fine linens and silver and china, and the food was as perfect as any they had ever eaten.

Lafitte would talk no business until after breakfast. That was not done in Louisiana, he told them. Business was not discussed while one was entertaining guests. Soon it was midday. Lafitte passed around cigars. Now he asked quietly the purpose of the gentlemen's visit.

Captain Lockyer presented him with a packet of important-looking documents. Lafitte untied the strings with which the papers were bound, unfolded the first one and began reading. This was signed by the commander of His Britannic Majesty's forces in the neighborhood. It was long and in flowery language, but it was a threatening and very strange document. It asked all Louisianians of French, Spanish and British blood to join with the English against the forces of the United States. If they did not, they would not only be attacked by His Majesty's ships, but the Indians in the vicinity would go on the warpath against them. The Indians were all with the English, it continued. Any house flying the flag of Great Britain would not be touched by them, nor would those flying flags of France and Spain.

The citizens had their choice. England was at war only with America. Neither her forces nor the Indians would harm loyal Englishmen, Frenchmen, and Spaniards.

Lafitte read this document twice and then laid it aside. He read the next. This was a letter addressed to "Mr. Lafitte or Commandant at Barataria." It asked for the services of the Baratarians against the Americans. It promised that Lafitte's property would not be harmed, nor that of any of his men. Furthermore, it offered Lafitte the rank of captain in the British Navy if he would help, and more land than he already owned.

There was a third letter and a fourth. The third asked Lafitte to guide Captain Lockyer throughout Barataria. It asked Lafitte to speak to all the men in the region and to instruct them that they were to aid the British. If any men did not care to do so, they must remain neutral. Lafitte was to join Captain W. H. Percy aboard His Majesty's Ship *Hermes* at Pensacola as soon as these matters had been accomplished. The fourth letter was even stronger and contained a direct warning. If Lafitte refused to aid the British they would destroy Barataria.

Lafitte put the letters down. So that was the way it was. Help destroy New Orleans or be destroyed. He hesitated. He knew the British were stronger than they had ever been before. He knew also what the Indians could do. He invited the Englishmen to have another glass of wine. He wanted to think, he told Captain Lockyer. He must have more time.

But Captain Lockyer insisted upon his answer at once. Perhaps he was suspicious of a trick. He leaned toward Lafitte and talked as to an old friend. Lafitte's answer must be to help the English. After all he was a Frenchman. The United States was not his country. Captain Lockyer offered even more than the rank of captain. Besides that, Lafitte would receive thirty thousand dollars when the war was won by the English.

The army officer, Captain McWilliams, also urged that Lafitte consent to help them. When America had been conquered, he said, Lafitte would have a great and honorable place. Had not Claiborne put a price on his head? Had not his brother, Pierre, been thrown into jail like a common criminal? Surely, Lafitte must hate the Americans, said McWilliams. The English had wonderful plans. They would sail up the Mississippi River and conquer the whole country. Part of their plan was to free the slaves, give them guns and set them against the white people. With the Indians and the slaves on their side, the British were certain to win. Then Lafitte would have more and more rewards. He would have more power than he had ever dreamed of.

Lafitte rose, smiling one of his rare smiles. "It is a perfect plan," he said. Then he bowed and added, "You must excuse me for a few minutes."

As he left the room and the house, the Englishmen talked among themselves. They were sure they had been successful. Lafitte would be on their side. With the help of the Baratarians, New Orleans would be easy to take. From there the British would sail up the river as conquerors. The war would be won.

They talked on and on. Then Captain Lockyer looked up. Men were filing into the room, bearded and mustached Baratarians, fierce-looking men with pistols in their hands and swords in their sashes. They surrounded the table where the Englishmen sat. The British officers rose, startled. The Baratarians seized them roughly, dragged them outside. On the beach in front of the house there were hundreds of other Baratarians, all of fearful appearance. In front of them stood Jean Lafitte, scowling darkly. The privateers set up terrifying shouts.

"Kill the English spies!" they shouted. "Turn them over to the Americans!"

Their elegant uniforms now torn and dirty, the British officers were pushed along the beach, thrust into the guardhouse and locked up. From outside there were still cries and threats. "Death to the British! We are Americans!"

The Englishmen were not kept locked up for long. Jean Lafitte appeared and turned the key in the lock with his own hand. He led the officers down the beach to their boat. Sweating and confused, the men crawled in. Before they began rowing toward their ship, Lafitte bowed politely.

"You see how my men feel," he said. "I must have more time to consider your offer."

The Englishmen began to row.

13: General Jackson Changes His Mind

IT WAS NOW THE AUTUMN OF 1814. A LITTLE aid had reached New Orleans from the Federal Government. A few American warships were in the harbor, and it was promised that General Andrew Jackson would arrive soon. Governor Claiborne breathed with a bit more ease, but he was still not sure he could save the city.

However, more help was within reach than Claiborne realized, and even when it first appeared he failed to recognize it. For soon after the attempt of the British to bribe him, Jean

Lafitte offered his services to the United States.

Lafitte had a friend in the Louisiana Legislature, a man named John Blanque. In September Blanque received two letters from Lafitte. One was addressed to Blanque himself, and another was enclosed to be read by Claiborne. These letters are absolute proof of Lafitte's loyalty to the United States.

In the letter to Blanque, Lafitte wrote that although condemned by his adopted country he would never allow anything to prevent him from "serving her or of proving that she has never ceased to be dear to me." Those were Lafitte's own words. Then he went on to describe the visit of the British officers.

In the letter to Claiborne, which was short and to the point, Lafitte made the same offer. He said, "This point of Louisiana, which I occupy, is of great importance in the present crisis. I tender my services to defend it." He made only one condition. He wanted pardons for himself and for all his men. He added, "I am a stray sheep, wishing to return to the sheepfold." At the end of the letter he told Claiborne that if he were refused the honor of fighting for the United States he would leave the country at once.

The letters gone, Lafitte waited for answers. During this time he wrote Captain Lockyer of the British forces. This letter was plainly a trick to fool the English. He apologized for their treatment at Grande Terre and again asked for more time.

But Lafitte waited in vain for Claiborne's answer. After Blanque took the letters to the Governor, Claiborne called a meeting of his naval and military advisors. He asked if they would accept help from Lafitte. The answer was no. Claiborne did not answer the letter.

Jean Lafitte wrote Blanque again, and again there was no reply. He even sent Blanque all the British papers that had been left with him, but this did no good either. Next, Pierre Lafitte wrote Blanque, offering his own services. The Baratarians waited. No answer came, at least not for some time.

When an answer came at last it could hardly have been the one expected by the Lafittes. For one morning at dawn a fleet of six American gunboats and the schooner *Carolina* appeared along the Gulf coastline. Lafitte's men came to him with warnings. They must resist the Americans, they said, if they were going to be attacked. Some of the men set up cannon and gathered arms and ammunition. Yet they waited, staring at the American flags.

This fleet was under the command of a Commodore Patterson of the United States Navy and Colonel J. Y. Ross of the Army. They had come to destroy the Baratarians, to wreck their hideouts, and to capture the leaders.

The Baratarians were powerful. Lafitte had a fleet of more than a dozen ships. His men could fight. Perhaps some of them wanted a battle when they realized why the Americans had come. Yet not a shot was fired by Lafitte's men.

As the American soldiers poured onto the beaches from the gunboats, Jean and Pierre Lafitte vanished. Many of the Baratarians broke and ran for the swamps, for Jean Lafitte's orders had gone out. As many as possible were to escape and hide, but there was to be no fighting. Out of the hundreds who were there, only eighty men were captured in the end. One of the prisoners taken back to New Orleans was Dominique You. He had refused to run and, roaring with laughter, had let himself be taken prisoner.

The soldiers went to work destroying Lafitte's possessions. Some of his ships were burned, some were taken away. Storehouses were ripped apart and the contents seized for the Government. Even Jean Lafitte's house was totally destroyed.

Commodore Patterson later reported that the American forces had captured seven schooners, a cruiser, and a felucca, as well as a half million dollars' worth of money and merchandise. He remarked that the force of the "pirates" numbered between eight hundred and a thousand men, but of these they had been able to take only eighty men prisoners. This was proof that the Baratarians had not tried to fight. The only damage they had done was to set two of their schooners on fire, rather than let them be captured.

As soon as it was all over Lafitte sent word to John Randolph Grymes and Edward Livingston, asking them to meet him in that same cottage where they had first talked with him about becoming the Lafittes' lawyers. The lawyers met him there several times. They began working as best they could to free Dominique You and the other Baratarians who were crowded into the calaboose.

Lafitte kept telling the lawyers he still wanted to fight for the United States. He knew that those men who had destroyed Barataria were not the whole country, he said. That was done by Claiborne's orders. Claiborne was ungrateful, Lafitte said, for he had already offered to help defend his country. Yet he would not blame the nation for what Claiborne had done.

Grymes and Livingston agreed with Lafitte. They were confident the Baratarians would yet be accepted. General Andrew Jackson was coming. He would not feel as Claiborne did, the lawyers told Lafitte. This gave him hope as the slow weeks passed.

Probably Jean Lafitte did not know that General Jackson already had formed an opinion of the Baratarians. Shortly after he received Lafitte's letter Governor Claiborne had sent it to Jackson at Mobile. The General wrote back and told Claiborne to have nothing to do with Lafitte or his men. Like Claiborne he called them "banditti" and "pirates."

General Jackson arrived in New Orleans on the second day of December. He and a half dozen of his officers rode to New Orleans from Mobile on horseback. "Old Hickory" had arrived.

Andrew Jackson was a tall, gaunt man, no longer young, but he still burned with the love of a good fight. He had been ill for some time before he reached New Orleans, but his eyes were hard and bright and his long jaw grim. He had come to the city to win the battle that everyone knew must come soon. He would win or die. Everyone understood that. Everyone felt better because he had come.

When Jackson walked into Claiborne's offices he was a startling sight. Everyone stared. Was this the great general? Why, he did not even wear a proper uniform! He had on an old leather cap, a torn and dirty blue Spanish cape, and high boots still caked with dried mud. The uniform he wore beneath the cape was almost ragged. He had been expected to appear in immaculate and colorful attire, with plumes in his hat and a glittering sword swinging at his side.

Yet the moment Jackson began to talk his listeners forgot his clothes as well as his thin, haggard face and the long gray hair that looked as if it hadn't been combed for weeks. At once they felt his strength and his fierce courage. His words were a strong tonic. Yes, with this old In dian fighter the city had a chance against the British. At least a chance. It was the first time anyone had felt that much hope.

At that conference, besides Governor Claiborne, were Commodore Patterson and Nicholas Girod, the mayor of New Orleans. Present, too, were Edward Livingston, who had known Jackson for many years, and John Randolph Grymes. Jackson told them he had come to defend the city, and to win. He would drive the English out of the whole territory, but he must have the help of all the citizens of New Orleans—French, Spanish and American. They must all work together, and with him. They must stop quarreling among themselves.

Jackson knew how different New Orleans was from other American cities. He knew that more than half its citizens did not yet consider themselves Americans at all, but Frenchmen or Spaniards. This feeling must end, he said. New Orleans was a part of the United States.

It is an interesting fact that the city's mayor Nicholas Girod, like many of the citizens, did not even understand English. Jackson's words had to be translated into French for him by Edward Livingston.

When the conference was nearly over someone mentioned Lafitte. It may have been Grymes, Livingston, or Governor Claiborne. Jackson had already written Claiborne what he thought of Jean Lafitte. Now he said it again. He wanted nothing to do with that bandit and pirate! Grymes and Livingston must have been disappointed.

After that, of course, there was a celebration in honor of Jackson's arrival. There was a huge reception and a parade through the streets. For these, Jackson appeared in a new uniform and looked like an entirely different man. Soon New Orleans realized that there were two Andrew Jacksons—the rough old Indian fighter, and a gentleman officer.

Livingston gave a large dinner party for the General and during the evening the ladies kept asking, "Is this your savage Indian fighter? Is this your rough frontier general?" In a few days Jackson was a great success in New Orleans.

Still in hiding, Jean Lafitte watched all this. And then he took one more chance. Jackson might accept him yet, if only he could get to see him.

Grymes and Livingston kept talking to Jackson, trying to get his promise to meet Lafitte in secret. But Jackson's answer was always the same. If he met that pirate it would be to arrest him and turn him over to Claiborne. New Orleans could be defended without the help of those Baratarians, he said.

Then, suddenly, he changed his mind. This may have been caused by a letter he received from Jean Lafitte. We don't know. Or it could have been Jackson's fiery and impulsive disposition that did it. Whatever the reason, one day he consented. He would meet the pirate. He sent word of this change of mind to Lafitte. Jean Lafitte came at once.

14: Jean Lafitte Meets Jackson and Claiborne

WHAT HAPPENED NEXT WAS ONE OF THE most important events in the long history of New Orleans. Jean Lafitte and General Jackson met in a secret place. Perhaps neither of them realized it, but upon the outcome of this meeting was to depend whether or not the city would continue to exist; for the British were boasting that after they took New Orleans they would burn it to the ground.

No one knows where this meeting was held. Some say that it was in Claiborne's offices in the

Cabildo. Some say that it was in a hidden room in a building on Bienville and Bourbon Streets which is now called the Old Absinthe House. Others say that it was in a room above the Exchange Coffee House on Chartres and St. Louis Streets, still others that it was in Jackson's headquarters on Royal Street. It isn't important where the meeting took place, but visitors to New Orleans today are shown them all, and that is why this is mentioned here.

Historians even disagree as to whether or not Claiborne was present. Some say he was, others that he was not; but he probably was there.

It is strange to think of Jean Lafitte sitting across a table from his old enemy, William Charles Cole Claiborne, but it is proof of how desperate was this moment. Otherwise, Claiborne would never have consented to meet Lafitte. But the most terrible enemies can unite and fight together when the common cause of all is threatened. Americans have done that all through the history of our country. So now Lafitte and Claiborne and Jackson began to bind themselves together in their common cause—to save New Orleans.

It is strange, too, that these three men were really much alike. All three were strong and forceful. All had high standards of honor. All were stubborn and had quick, fiery tempers. So all seemed to understand each other. Jackson and Lafitte seemed to have liked each other on sight. Later, when Jackson spoke of Lafitte or mentioned him in his letters, he never again called him a bandit or a pirate.

Jackson had been working hard since the day he arrived in the city, His own troops had now reached the city, his Tennessee regulars and Mississippi dragoons, veterans of battles with the British at Pensacola and with the Indians at Mobile. They were a rugged, experienced lot, well-trained, but badly armed and poorly clothed. The British, wearing their own splendid bright red coats, were afterwards to call them "dirty shirts."

Besides these, Jackson had little to start with in New Orleans. There were Commodore Patterson's gunboats, and Colonel Ross had an army of 700 regulars and a militia of about 1,000 men. There were some forts near the city, all of them in bad condition—Fort St. John, Fort St. Philip, Fort St. Charles and Fort Petites Coquilles, the last a new one just being built. These were already being reconditioned.

Jackson had ordered all bayous between New Orleans and the Gulf of Mexico blocked. He had begun training Ross's men. But there was not much time. The British, under General Sir Edward Pakenham, were already approaching Chandeleur Island. Pakenham and his fleet had sailed from Jamaica toward the mouth of the Mississippi River six days before Jackson had reached New Orleans. There were at least 12,000 seasoned fighting men under Pakenham's command. The Americans were terribly outnumbered no matter what they did.

But the worst of Jackson's troubles was the lack of arms and ammunition. His army had almost no flints, without which their guns would be useless. This lack of flints seemed a problem that could not be solved.

Jean Lafitte solved it. Jackson needed flints? He should have them. There were still many guns and muskets hidden away in the swamps, Lafitte said. These arms had not been found by the soldiers who had destroyed or taken away so much Baratarian property. Moreover, there were 7,500 flints. They were General Jackson's. Jackson accepted them with gratitude. Upon them might depend the outcome of the battle soon to begin.

Lafitte also gave information to Jackson and Claiborne. His Baratarians knew much of the movements of the British fleet and of those troops which had already landed in the swamps. The Baratarians were expert spies. They could move through the marshes and along the bayous as quietly and as secretly as Indians. The English found the region difficult to cross. For the Baratarians it was like playing in their own back yard.

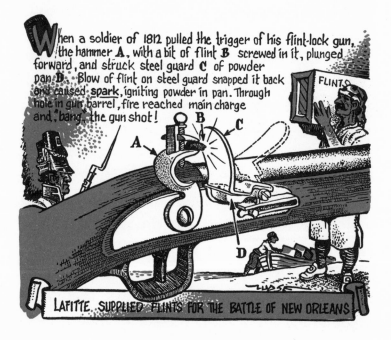

When a soldier of 1812 pulled the trigger of his flint-lock gun, the hammer **A**, with a bit of flint **B** screwed in it, plunged forward, and struck steel guard **C** of powder pan **D**. Blow of flint on steel guard snapped it back and caused spark, igniting powder in pan. Through hole in gun barrel, fire reached main charge and, "bang," the gun shot!

FLINTS

LAFITTE SUPPLIED FLINTS FOR THE BATTLE OF NEW ORLEANS

But the Baratarians wanted to do more than that, Lafitte told Jackson and Claiborne. They wanted to fight. They could not come out of hiding if they were to be treated as outlaws, condemned as criminals. Even now, he reminded them, eighty of his men, including Dominique You, one of his lieutenants, were locked up in cells in the Cabildo. These were excellent fighting men. There were hundreds, more than a thousand more like them, all in hiding along the bayous and lakes of Barataria.

Jackson listened. When the conference ended the sky was bright with morning.

15: Pirate Turned Patriot

THE MEETING WAS A COMPLETE SUCCESS. THE
next day the doors of the cells in the Cabildo
swung open and Dominique You and the other
imprisoned privateers walked out into freedom.
All joined Jackson's army at once. During the following day or two there was a steady stream of
Baratarians pouring into the city to enlist.

The sight of all these men coming out of the
swamps and appearing by the hundreds in the

streets of the small city must have been exciting to the citizens of New Orleans. There were men of every kind and of every nationality—American, French, Spanish, Slavic, and mixtures of every race. There were dark men with thick beards and frightening mustaches. There were slim Louisiana youths, some of them the sons of wealthy planters, who had joined the forces of Lafitte for adventure. There were men who wore kerchiefs about their heads and gold hoops in their ears and looked exactly as pirates are supposed to look. All of them brought their weapons with them—guns and pistols, swords and knives and cutlasses.

Their appearance frightened some of the citizens of New Orleans. They had been warned about these men for years. They had been told that the Baratarians were thieves and thugs, cutthroats and murderers. Now they walked about freely, not only untouched by the city officials, but under their protection and guidance. These men had come to help save New Orleans. The pirates had become patriots.

But the marshes were by no means emptied. Once enlisted under the United States flag and General Jackson, many of the men were sent

back to the banks of the lakes and bays and bayous to guard them against the coming of the
British. Much danger existed there, and the British had already begun activities that would lead
to the attack upon New Orleans.

Dominique You and Beluche were experienced artillerists. Jackson assigned them at once.
They were put at the head of divisions of artillery and allowed to pick from the Baratarians
the men they wanted to serve under them.
Others of the privateers were sent to the various
forts—Forts St. John, St. Philip, Petites Coquilles
and the others.

In these early days of the struggle Jean and
Pierre Lafitte spent much time with Jackson, as
the plans were laid. Early in December Jackson
declared New Orleans under martial law. Cur-
fews were established, which meant the citizens
must keep off the streets after dark. Soldiers were
on guard everywhere. Jackson urged all citizens
to join in the defense. At first there was not too
much response to this. Shoulders were shrugged.
All Orleanians were worried, but this was an
American war, and they did not all feel yet that
they were Americans.

Soon Jackson had defenses set up all through

the Barataria region—at Last Island, which was the last of the larger islands stretching out into the Gulf, at Grand Isle, and at Grande Terre. Defenses were even set up at The Temple which, at least for a time, was under the command of Jean Lafitte. Lafitte was now defending the very spot where he had held his great auctions, and he was doing it for the United States. The change was complete.

But even with all these precautions the British managed to pour into Barataria and to move closer and closer to New Orleans. There were so many waterways and routes that they could not all be defended by Jackson's small forces.

On December 10, 1814 British frigates attempted to enter Lake Borgne and land on Chandeleur Island. Lake Borgne is very shallow, so the English had to leave their frigates and take to forty-five small open boats. Five American gunboats scouting in the lake attacked them, and were defeated! It was a terrible loss to the small American sea power in the region.

The British moved on to the mainland and within a week put 7,000 men ashore at Villeré Plantation, only nine miles outside of New Orleans.

Villeré Plantation was the property of General Villeré. There the general and his two sons were surprised by a detachment of British. The family, together with a small company of militia, were captured. Only one of the sons, Major Gabriel Villeré, escaped. He jumped from a window and hid behind a huge live oak tree until he was able to flee toward New Orleans and Jackson's headquarters. This was on the afternoon of December 23rd.

General Jackson was startled at the news Major Villeré brought him. He had known the British were close, but not as close as this! He had hoped for at least another day or two. Now he did not have even that. He gathered his aides immediately and when they were all together he rose and faced them with a grave expression.

"Gentlemen," he said, "the British are below the city! We must fight them tonight."

Jackson assigned his officers at once. They were to break camp and move on to positions he directed. General Carroll headed a contingent to Bayou Bienvenu. General Coffee and his Tennesseans were to close in upon the enemy at Villeré Plantation by moving toward its flank and rear through the swamps. A group of picked volunteers, many of Lafitte's men among them, were instructed to edge along the river. Governor Claiborne, now in active service as a fighting man, headed a corps at the Gentilly Road, which led into New Orleans.

The schooner *Carolina,* under the command of Commodore Patterson, weighed anchor and moved swiftly down the Mississippi. The instructions to Patterson were to anchor near the British encampment and signal for the attack by firing a broadside of hot shot. Lafitte was on duty at The Temple with a group of his Baratarians.

When all orders were delivered Jackson lay down upon a sofa. He rested but thirty minutes. He was still a sick man, suffering from malarial fever, and this had been one of his worst days. He felt it would be a long time before he closed his eyes again and he was right. He was not to sleep for the next seventy hours. That same afternoon he was on horseback reviewing his troops as they passed.

As news of the British advance spread New Orleans at last became excited. A detachment of young Creoles ran all the way from Fort St. John to New Orleans to join Jackson. The streets became filled with people. Boys of sixteen and younger and men over sixty were enlisting for service. Nationality and race became of no importance. Everyone wanted to help in the struggle. In this final hour, nothing but defending New Orleans mattered and word that the enemy was now nine miles below the city at the Villeré Plantation had brought the citizens together.

As at all such times everyone wanted work to do, to be part of all the activity. Women waved flags, French and American. They stood on the balconies in the narrow streets and cheered the men passing beneath. When Lafitte's men passed great cries of praise were heard. There were Dominique You and Beluche and their cannon. Even Gambi was there, and hundreds of others —bearded, swarthy, oddly-dressed fellows, who had been called pirates. No one feared them now. They were heroes.

The people sang. They sang the *Marseillaise*, the national anthem of France, and *Yankee Doodle.* They lined the streets and gave the men presents—food to take with them, bread and wine, weapons that had been kept in families for many years. And all the men wanted to get into the fight together—whites, blacks, and red Indians, too. For in spite of the boasts of the British not all the Indians were on their side. Eighteen Choctaw Indians formed a team of their own and sped down the river to join in the attack.

Of course there was fear in people's hearts, too. The dreadful rumors were repeated. Some of them contradicted the others. The British were going to give New Orleans back to Spain, some said. No, said others, the city would be looted and then destroyed by fire. Older citizens remembered those other fires the city had gone through and shuddered. All women and children would be killed, some people said. The British would have no mercy. Probably much of this was exaggerated, but at the time it was believed by many of the citizens. With almost all the men on their way to join up with General Jackson, the women gathered in groups in certain houses, their children with them. People prayed in the churches. There was both excitement and terror.

All this time Jackson sat upon his horse and reviewed his troops as they filed past. What a strange army it was! Few had proper uniforms, or even proper weapons. Some of the men wore clothes too fine and entirely unsuited for battles. Others were almost in rags. Many carried their own weapons—rifles, muskets, pistols and swords, anything that could be used in a fight.

Jackson saw his two regiments of regulars— the only men marching who could boast of much experience at war. There were hundreds of Baratarians, tough and rugged to be sure, but few with any army training. There were the tall, lean Kentuckians, flatboatmen, used to brawling but not to organized warfare. They wanted to fight for New Orleans and Louisiana because it was now a part of the United States. There were slim Frenchmen, skilled at duelling, but looking out of place here. There were Germans and Irishmen, farmers, fishermen, trappers. There were companies of Negroes. There was a scattering of Indians, besides the eighteen Choctaws.

They marched bravely past General Jackson, sometimes singing, sometimes in silence. All the way along the streets people continued to sing with them or cheer them as they passed. But everyone knew what they faced, the great odds against the highly trained English troops. It is doubtful if a braver little army ever marched in the history of the world.

Altogether they numbered 2,131 men. The British were known to have at least 12,000. Less

than half of Jackson's men had been to war before. All the British were veterans of many cam-
paigns in many different places.

Jackson's men began leaving the city at about
three o'clock on the afternoon of that December
23rd. As they moved down the road and came a
little closer to the British encampment, nine
miles from the city, they began to find signs
posted along fences and trees. These read:

**LOUISIANIANS, REMAIN QUIET IN
YOUR HOMES; YOUR SLAVES SHALL
BE PRESERVED TO YOU, AND YOUR
PROPERTY RESPECTED. WE MAKE
WAR ONLY AGAINST AMERICANS.**

The British did not yet know that the citizens
of Louisiana and of New Orleans were rapidly
becoming Americans and that they were ready
to fight for America, to the death if necessary.
Some of them were already on their way to do so.

16: The Battle of New Orleans

BRITISH TROOPS ENCAMPED ON THE VILLERÉ
Plantation saw the *Carolina* glide into view on
the Mississippi River at about seven o'clock on
December 23rd. It was already dark, but her
lines were silhouetted against the sky. The British
took her for an ordinary merchant vessel, and
therefore were not disturbed even when she was
hailed by sentries and no reply came from the
ship.

The *Carolina* sheered close to shore and anchored silently. A hundred exhausted but curious Englishmen crept closer to the water's edge to watch. Suddenly, from the deck, came the loud voice of Captain Henley, serving under Commodore Patterson as the ship's master. "Now, boys," he shouted, "give it to them for the honor of America!"

Heavy fire opened at once, pouring from the *Carolina's* starboard batteries and small arms. The enemy, realizing quickly what this meant, returned the attack. But only for forty minutes. After that they had other things to worry about.

For the broadside from the *Carolina* was the signal for Jackson's forces, already concealed on every side of the British. They leapt upon the British through the darkness, guns blazing, wild yells cutting through the night.

It was a complete surprise to the British. They were so stunned that afterwards a British officer, Major General Keane, reported to General Pakenham that there had been three American ships on the river. In reality there was only the *Carolina,* but she made a noise like three.

A moment later the British were engaged in intense fighting on the land. Jackson's forces struck swiftly and terribly. Soon fighting was in progress not only on the Villeré Plantation, but on the Lacoste Plantation and the De la Ronde Plantation which adjoined it.

The American Seventh Regiment, under Lieutenant McKlennand, began a drive against the enemy's outposts on the high road near the river. Colonel de la Ronde, the owner of one of the three plantations, guided General Coffee and 600 men against the British right flank. Major d'Aquin's battalion of colored men and the loyal Choctaws attacked from the left. The Tennesseans with their famous rifles came up from the orange tree groves on the De la Ronde Plantation and inflicted huge losses upon the enemy. Dominique You and Beluche and their artillery opened fire from their posts on the levee along the river.

There was much hand-to-hand fighting, and in the midst of it all, General Jackson wheeled about on horseback, no longer seeming ill and fever-ridden, his deep voice booming encouragement to his men, his eyes bright, his own pistol cracking.

It was all over shortly after nine o'clock when the *Carolina* silenced her guns. Minutes later the the British retreated and fled through a hole in the American lines. A little later all was quiet. To aid the British a heavy fog had descended and General Jackson, knowing that neither the Americans nor the British could see each other and had already begun to kill their own comrades, decided the Americans would attack no more that night. The Americans camped on the Lacoste Plantation, the British not far away on the Villeré Plantation, although they were driven to its backlands.

Up to this point it was a complete American victory. The British had been surprised and 400 of· them killed. The Americans had lost only twenty-four men. Both sides had taken prisoners, but the Americans had captured many more than the enemy.

More important, perhaps, the British had lost heart, although the Americans did not know that yet. The British had believed that the French Louisianians would refuse to fight at the side of the Americans. During the height of the fighting many shots and cries in French had been heard. The British knew now that they were not to take New Orleans easily, if at all.

Jackson said later that he was extremely pleased with his men. Their courage had been beyond his expectations. And now they had all tasted battle.

But Jackson did not sleep that night. He met with his officers and with Dominique You, Beluche, and Pierre Lafitte. Jean Lafitte alone was missing, for he was still down at The Temple. Jackson and the others spent the whole foggy night planning the continuation of the fighting.

Toward dawn Jackson and most of his men moved two miles back toward the city, behind the Rodriguez Canal. He was still outnumbered and he knew American victory depended greatly upon caution. Every man must count, every shot. An attack by daylight might bring defeat, but no attack came. There were only small skirmishes between isolated groups of Britishers and Americans.

Later, Jean Lafitte came up from The Temple and met with Jackson and his officers. Small contingents of British had been beaten back in numerous places in Barataria, Lafitte reported.

General Jackson began a report to be sent to Washington. In it he called Lafitte and his Baratarians "privateers and gentlemen." He no longer called them "banditti and pirates!"

On December 26th bad news reached Jackson.

His scouts reported that the British were landing more troops at Chef Menteur, not far from where the other British were stationed. The enemy was also busy erecting a battery along the river at Villeré Plantation for the purpose of attacking the *Carolina*. The *Carolina* had moved to the other side of the wide river and anchored. There she had, on the 25th, been joined by the *Louisiana,* another American ship.

Jackson ordered the levee cut at Jumonville Plantation below the British camp, hoping the river would rush in and drown or drive out the enemy. This failed. The river was not high enough and the British suffered no damage.

On December 27th British fire opened against the *Carolina,* which was unable to move upstream because of high winds. The vessels returned the attack with blazing guns, but within fifteen minutes the *Carolina* was in flames and her crew had to leave ship. The *Louisiana,* also a British target, was towed up river out of the range of the English cannons and saved. Unfortunately, the gallant *Carolina* burned to the water's edge, its hull sank slowly out of sight, and it was gone forever.

The next day came the awaited British land

attack upon the Americans at Rodriguez Canal. It began at dawn with the firing of several pieces of British artillery upon the American lines and also upon the *Louisiana,* now anchored in the river near the American formations.

Jackson's forces had only five pieces of battery at this engagement, but those artillerists, Dominique You and Beluche, directed a terrific return fire and the *Louisiana,* after allowing the British columns to advance within range, opened fire with all her guns. The enemy columns broke at once and retreated rapidly. They had lost nearly three hundred men. Jackson lost only seven men. It was another quick and amazing victory.

On December 29th, having lost the *Carolina,* Commodore Patterson brought down the river a new twenty-four pounder. The following day this new ship and the *Louisiana* opened fire on the British all along the river levees. The British retreated with speed and with more and even heavier losses than before. Night after night the two ships continued to pound away.

Meanwhile both sides received reinforcements. The British commander, General Sir Edward Pakenham, until now still encamped in the swamps, arrived to take command, bringing with him several thousand additional troops. Jackson's forces were joined by about 2,300 Kentuckians under the command of Major General John Thomas and Brigadier General John Adair. Unfortunately, however, only about 700 of these Kentuckians were armed. The Baratarians supplied what they could, but even this was not enough.

For several days there were no major engagements, although the Americans continued to fight in their own way. There was constant attack upon the English in what we would now call guerilla warfare, especially by the Tennesseans with their famous rifles. Tennessee rifles brought death and dismay to the English day and night. Dressed in their brown homespun tunics, dirty and ragged, the dreaded "dirty shirts," as the English called them, crept like snakes through tall grass and ditches to pick off British sentries and small groups of English soldiers. The Tennesseans called this kind of fighting "hunting parties" and they carried on with them constantly, until the English feared them almost more than any other part of the American troops.

We must remember that wars in those days were quite different from wars today. The British fought according to the European customs of the time. Gallant and brave, they marched to battle in formation, often to the beating of drums, their red coats brilliant in the sun and visible even on moonlit nights. The red coats made them fine targets, as they advanced shoulder to shoulder.

The Americans did not fight that way. They fought from trenches and ditches and from behind any sort of barricades they could erect. They fired upon the English from clumps of bushes and from trees into which they had climbed. The British complained that the American type of fighting was uncivilized and against the rules of warfare. The Americans replied that they were fighting for their country, their homes, their lives, and their families. It was the British who had invaded *their* country. Therefore they had only one duty—to kill as many English as possible and in any way possible.

During the night of December 31st, word reached Jackson that the British were building batteries along a ditch at Chalmette Plantation, not far from his lines. Jackson came out of the house he was now occupying on the first morning of the new year and saw that one of the heavy fogs had arisen during the night. Some of his scouts, Baratarians and Tennesseans, told him the closest British battery was only six hundred yards away, but the fog was so dense it was impossible to take any action against it. A man couldn't see more than five feet at this hour.

The British waited until ten o'clock and opened a heavy cannonade. Jackson consulted with his officers, the Lafittes and Dominique You. The Americans retreated slightly. British shells and cannon balls struck Jackson's headquarters and the house burst into flame. American guns returned the fire, but Jackson's forces had only ten cannon now, while the British had twenty-eight, so other means were put to use.

As enemy fire decreased the sharpshooters went out upon their hunting parties—Tennesseans with their dreaded rifles and Baratarians, also expert at this kind of fighting. Every time a redcoat appeared through the wisps of fog that still lingered a rifle cracked. Sometimes several Baratarians fell upon small groups of English with drawn knives. By darkness this engagement was ended, although the American guerillas continued to linger close to enemy lines, striking whenever they had a chance.

During the night of January 3rd General

Jackson was told that a division of English were planning an attack upon his rear flank. The enemy was landing from boats at Bayou Bienvenu and the Piernas Canal. Jackson sent two hundred men under General Coffee with orders to attack these invaders and drive them into the bayou. It was now raining heavily and the men sank knee-deep in mud, but they slugged along for hours. When they reached Bayou Bienvenu there were no enemy in sight. The report had been a false one.

There were other reports, some true, some rumors or lies spread by the enemy to waste the Americans' strength. Jackson had to have every report investigated. He felt the largest part of the fighting was still ahead and he could not afford to take any chances.

The British prisoners sometimes talked. On January 6th Jackson learned from some of these, captured the day before by Pierre Lafitte and a group of his Baratarians, that the English were digging out Canal Villeré. This ran through the Villeré Plantation to the river. The British planned to use the channel as a passage for their boats. Scouts who were sent out reported that Canal Villeré was the scene of much activity.

English soldiers and sailors were digging and pushing small boats through the shallow water. Some regiments were kept drilling. Pakenham was reviewing others. Jackson waited.

Jackson felt that now the big fight was coming. The next evening he was even more certain. With the help of telescopes his officers saw English soldiers making scaling ladders. British officers rode about, stopping at different posts as if they were delivering orders. Troops marched about. Pickets and sentries had been increased. Even the sounds of the Britishers' preparations could be heard—the strokes of hammers, the raised voices. The British were about to attack!

There was quiet in the American camp, the silence that usually is noticeable before a great battle. Jackson was well pleased with all his men. He had more faith in them now and more hope for victory than ever before. It was true that they were existing under miserable conditions. It rained most of the time. They slept in the mud in the best way they could. They had little food besides stale hard bread. They were poorly and thinly clothed, although they were better off in this regard than they had been. Recently they had received hundreds of cloaks, pantaloons, shirts and shoes, all made by the women of New Orleans from blankets and other woolens donated to the ladies for this purpose by the State Legislature.

Despite all these drawbacks, Jackson knew his men were now a unit. As weak as they might look, they were really strong. They would fight to win and they would fight together. If the British ever reached New Orleans they would have to march over the Americans' dead bodies.

As dawn broke on January 8th there was a beginning of movement in the English camp. This was the start of what most historians call the Battle of New Orleans. Actually, the battle *for* New Orleans had begun on December 23rd.

Jackson ordered a quiet advance of some of his men. Observation showed the British occupying two-thirds of the space between the two camps. Then a British Congreve rocket went up. This was their signal for attack. An American battery replied with a burst of fire.

At once the British appeared and gave three loud cheers. Then they began marching toward the Americans slowly and with measured steps, sixty men abreast, the morning sun on their red coats. Some of the British soldiers carried scaling ladders with which they intended to climb the American fortifications.

One of Jackson's batteries, under the command of Garrigues Flaugeac, let loose at them with cannon. The English went down quickly, line after line of them. More kept coming. Tennesseans and Baratarians let them have blasts of rifleshot. The British continued to come. In a few minutes the battlefield was covered with English dead and dying.

The Americans continued a blaze of fire from entrenchments, from their five small batteries (two of them under the commands of Dominique You and Beluche) and from the rifles of Tennesseans, Kentuckians, and Baratarians behind their crude barricades of earthwork supported by boards and reinforced with cotton bales. In some places these barricades were five feet high and twenty feet thick. The first damage came to them when British shot set fire to the cotton bales. These had to be dragged from their positions by the Americans to prevent the entire fortification from going up in flames.

As English soldiers dropped from their columns others were rushed in to fill the gaps. Officers could be seen riding about ordering the men into formation. The column swerved from what had been a march toward Flaugeac's battery, but it moved forward at its same pace, following all the rules of courteous European warfare. However, this did not last long. As English dead strewed the ground the column began to quaver and break. First it increased its speed, then it broke entirely and the slow parade was over.

Before American fire that seemed a solid sheet of flame the English became confused. Officers rushed forward to try to stop their soldiers from fleeing, but nothing could halt them now. They ran for their lives, although their officers shouted and begged them to go on fighting and even beat them with the flats of their swords. In the middle of it all General Sir Edward Pakenham, their commander-in-chief, trying to rally his forces for continued attack upon the Americans, fell mortally wounded and died.

When the British had crept back into the woods and the ditches for the rest of the day General Jackson walked among his troops to congratulate them upon this greatest of their victories. There was quiet again behind the American barricade. Men sat around fires in order to warm themselves against the wet and bitter cold.

Some of them were making coffee from a supply of it that had just arrived the day before. Jackson would accept a cup of the hot drink, murmur a few words of encouragement and move on. He stopped and talked to the Lafittes. Their Baratarians were fine fighters, the old general said. Those gentlemen had his admiration.

There is a story that Jackson also paused to speak with tough old Dominique You at his battery. According to the tale, the General stopped and sniffed the coffee Dominique was brewing.

"That smells good," said the General. "It is better coffee than we get. Where did it come from? Did you *smuggle* it in?"

Dominique You shrugged, grinned up at Jackson. "That may be," he said. He turned to the Baratarian beside him. "Fill up a cup for the General," he told him.

Sitting beside them, Jackson drank the coffee. Then he turned to the aide accompanying him on his rounds of the men. "You know," he said, "if I were ordered to storm the gates of Hell, with Captain Dominique as my lieutenant, I would have no misgivings of the result!" With that compliment left behind him Jackson strode away.

17: *The End of the Struggle*

THE FIGHTING ON THE MORNING OF JANUARY 8th lasted only one hour. By nine-thirty it was over. The Americans had only thirteen men killed and wounded. The British, amazing as it seems, had lost 2,600! All fighting between Americans and Englishmen in the region was not yet over, but there no longer seemed to be any question of who would win.

On the field of Chalmette, panic had swept

the British. Many of the officers continued attempts to rouse the men to new fighting, but it
was hopeless. Something had gone out of them.
The English soldiers had met a type of fighting
that was different from any they had seen before
and they had no defenses against it.

In the cruel Napoleonic wars, at the Crimea,
the British had advanced in their neat formations, in their beautiful uniforms, the glory of
battle in their hearts, as they had today, and they
had won either victory or the honorable position
of having given a good fight. Here at Chalmette
they had not even given a good fight. They had
been defeated miserably by a force much smaller
than their own and much inferior in arms—or at
least in number of arms. They had been defeated
by men without their experience, who did not
fight as the British thought soldiers were supposed to fight.

The death of General Pakenham was perhaps
the worst of their shocks. Pakenham was the
brother-in-law of Wellington, who had defeated
Napoleon, and he had been promised the coro-
net of an earl if he captured Louisiana. It was
hard for his men to believe he had been killed
by these "pirates and dirty shirts."

The battlefield was a place of horror, thick with British dead, dying and wounded. At last the Americans could not stand the groans and screams of the enemy injured. Some of them left their barricades and tried to reach some of the wounded to give them treatment. But when the British fired on them, the Americans had to let the wounded lie where they were.

While all this was taking place Americans stationed across the river from Chalmette, under the command of General David Morgan, were attacked by British. The red-coated troops had crossed the river in the boats they had brought through the Canal Villeré to the Mississippi. General Morgan's men, most of them Kentuckians, were badly armed and outnumbered. They fought as long as possible and then retreated. Their retreat made it an English victory. Yet the losses suffered by the British made it an American victory, for the Americans lost only one man and the British 120. In spite of this, Jackson considered the retreat a mistake and he withdrew Morgan from command.

On the evening of the 8th the wounded began reaching New Orleans, five miles from Chalmette. These were both American and English, and the women of the city took them in their care and did what could be done for them.

That night there was silence at Chalmette. The next morning Jackson received a message from Lambert, the new British commander, suggesting that both sides do no more shooting until they had buried their dead. Jackson agreed. Then men of both sides mingled on the battlefield picking up the bodies, talking freely. Jackson had some of his men deliver the bodies of three officers of the British army who had been killed on the American breastworks. All this seems curious to us now, for we do not make war in that way any more.

During the same day, however, there was activity in another spot not far away. Early on the morning of the 9th, American officers at Fort St. Philip below New Orleans saw five English ships in the Mississippi River. The vessels—two bombships, one sloop, one brig and one schooner— were anchored two and a quarter miles from the fort. A pair of barges sent from the vessels, sailed to within a mile and a half of the fort and began sounding the depths of the river.

Immediately the batteries at the fort opened fire and the barges retreated. Then the enemy blazed away at the fort with four sea-mortars. They continued the attack for eight days, damaging the fort badly, but killing only two men. The guns at Fort St. Philip were powerless to reply, for they could not reach the distant British ships. It seemed for a while that the British would capture the fort, but on the morning of the ninth day the enemy pulled out and retreated. They had not dared to come closer to the American guns.

Scattered firing was resumed at Chalmette as soon as the dead were buried, but there were no more real attempts by the British to approach the American barricades. In the meantime there was fighting in Barataria.

Jean Lafitte was down at The Temple with a company of his Baratarians. On several occasions the British opened fire, but the privateers, fighting under their fierce leader's command, drove them away each time. The chênière, with its tall thick trees and mounds of shells, was a natural fort, and the Englishmen, strangers in these swamps, could not approach it. With The Temple conquered, many more British troops might have reached New Orleans or Chalmette.

Commodore Patterson sent six boats to Lake

Borgne on January 10th. These were new ships, well-armed and carrying crews of tough fighting men, that had just reached New Orleans. In a battle with three British transports, all the British ships were captured and the men made American prisoners.

Back at Chalmette, Jackson and his forces knew the end had almost come. The British could not fight any longer. More and more were deserting now. Their spirit was gone.

On the 15th of January an Englishman, deserting to the American lines, told Jackson that the British were getting ready to retreat. The Americans waited. Two days later, on the 17th, General Lambert asked General Jackson by messenger if he would be willing to exchange prisoners. Jackson's reply was that he would exchange them man for man. The British then sent him the sixty-three men the British had captured and Jackson returned sixty-three British prisoners. But the Americans were still holding several hundred more Englishmen.

That evening the Americans opened fire on the British again with heavy mortars. The British did not return the fire, and there was no sign of movement on their side.

On the morning of the 19th an unusual silence was noticed on the British side of the battlefield. Had they gone? Jackson and his officers turned telescopes toward the British encampment. They could see red-coated sentries standing very still at their posts. British flags rippled in the morning breeze. Yet there was something strange about it all, something that was not natural. Old General Humbert, the Frenchman who had invited Lafitte to his birthday dinner, said he thought the British had gone.

"How can you be certain?" Jackson asked him.

"Never mind," General Humbert said. "There is no one there. They left during the night."

"It may be a trick," Jackson told him. "What about those sentries we can see from here?"

"Watch that crow," said Humbert.

As Jackson and the other officers watched, a crow circled over the sentries and then settled on one of them. Humbert laughed. "Did you ever see a crow do that before?" he asked.

Then the Americans knew that Lambert and his men had gone. No crow will perch on a living man. When they reached the British camp they found it empty except for some Englishmen too badly wounded to be moved. A note from the British general asked Jackson to see that these men were cared for. The "sentries" were merely British uniforms stuffed with grass and weeds and tied in their places like scarecrows!

Some of the Americans went after the British, but there was little action. Eight Englishmen were taken prisoners. The rest escaped to Lake Borgne. Here they were again attacked, and again they retreated, almost without fighting. They continued to retreat through the marshes until they reached the Gulf of Mexico. Then Jackson received a letter from Lambert. There would be no more attempts to take New Orleans, wrote the British commander. He and his forces were leaving the region forever.

The Battle of New Orleans was over! The Americans had not only won, but they had won by gigantic odds. It was a glorious victory for Jackson and all his men. Before breaking his lines for the return to New Orleans, Jackson thanked each company. "The enemy has retreated," he said, "and your general has now leisure to proclaim to the world what he has

noticed with admiration and pride—your un-
daunted courage, your patriotism, and your
patience under hardships and fatigue."

He said much more. Here were men of every
kind, he told them, different even in the languages they spoke, fighting together as one. He
was very proud. They had done much more than
he expected, under conditions that had seemed
impossible. They had saved not only New
Orleans, but possibly the Union. At the end of
his talk he thanked God for their success.
Heaven had been with them.

Yet, as he led his men from Chalmette, Jackson took no chances. He left a regiment of
Louisiana militia at the Villeré Plantation and
a detachment of Kentuckians at the Lacoste
Plantation. Several smaller parties were sent to
scout Lake Borgne and other sections of Barataria to make sure no British lingered in that
neighborhood. United States vessels were instructed to continue watch on the Mississippi
River, and the forts were kept well staffed. But
nothing more occurred. It was really over.

Just before leaving camp General Jackson
wrote a full report to the Secretary of War in

Washington. In it he praised all the divisions of men who had helped him win—the Tennesseans and the Kentuckians, together with their rifles, the brave Louisiana Creoles, and the colored troops that had fought brilliantly under Major d'Aquin. Coming to the Baratarians, Jackson wrote: "The brothers Lafitte have exhibited the same courage and fidelity; and the General promises that the Government shall be duly appraised of their conduct."

This was high praise indeed from Andrew Jackson to the Lafittes. It meant that the General would see to it that never again, while he was in Louisiana, would the Lafittes be considered outlaws.

Jackson also gave special praise to other Baratarians, writing:

"Captains Dominique and Beluche, lately commanding privateers at Barataria, with part of their former crews and many brave citizens of New Orleans, were stationed at Batteries Nos. 3 and 4. The General cannot avoid giving his warm approbation of the manner in which these gentlemen have uniformly conducted themselves while under his command, and of the gallantry with which they have redeemed the pledge they gave at the opening of the campaign to defend the country."

The report completed and all other matters settled, Jackson gave his order, and the heroes of Chalmette began the five-mile march back to the city they had saved and which now waited to honor them.

18: Lafitte the Hero

OF COURSE THERE HAD BEEN MUCH EXCITE-
ment and terror in the city while the fighting
was going on. No ablebodied men were left behind in New Orleans except the few who made
up a small guard. There were only women, old
men and children. All of them expected the
worst if the battle were to be lost and the British
enter the city. It was common talk that the city
would be destroyed and those remaining within
it either be killed or driven out without any
possessions.

There had been terrible days and nights. Some of the ladies even carried daggers in their belts and sashes, saying that they would fight too, if they had to do so. They clung together desperately with their children, trembling with fear.

The rumors grew, as they always do in any city which may be invaded by an enemy at any moment. The news the people received was almost always bad, or else it simply could not be believed. Now and then they heard the cannons roar from the plantation battlefields. Women and children and old sick men sat behind closed shutters with rifles or muskets in their hands, waiting to hear horses' hoofs and see redcoats appear in their own street. For some of them it must have seemed the end of everything they loved, the end of their lives. They heard the British had come in such numbers and were so well armed that the defenders of New Orleans could do nothing but fight to the death.

The most dreadful day was January 8th, the day of the struggle known as the Battle of New Orleans, when the British had attacked for that single hour at dawn and been defeated utterly. The evening before a messenger from Chalmette had told the citizens of the city that the battle

was about to begin. That night extra preparations were made. The women and children gathered into even tighter groups than usual. A
hundred of them were at the house of a Madame
Porée at the corner of Royal and Dumaine
Streets, for instance. That house still exists.
A famous historian of New Orleans, Charles
Gayarré, then a small boy, was there with his
mother, and he wrote about that night many
years later.

Everyone stayed awake all night. The ladies
thought the British might wipe out the Americans by morning and come galloping into the
city by daybreak. They were only five miles
away. Some of the women were brave, but others
cried all night. A few even fainted, but no one
had time to bother with them. Gayarré said they
would faint and revive without anyone's paying
any attention to them. Then they would faint
again. That went on all night long.

At dawn they heard the cannons. That frightened the women even more. The booming of big
guns meant that fighting was going on, and of
course there was no way for the people in New
Orleans to tell what was happening. Nowadays
if a city were about to be invaded that way it

might be possible to take out some of the women and children, but there was no way then. There was nothing to do but wait. They barred the shutters tight at the windows and they prayed.

It was past noon when a horseman came galloping into Royal Street. He stopped at each corner and shouted, "Victory! Victory!" Shutters flew open and the women and children ran out upon the balconies that hung over the sidewalks. At Madame Porée's house there was great excitement when the cry came, "Victory! Victory!"

After that there was not much fear in New Orleans. The fighting continued, but everyone felt that the British were beaten. The news grew better each day. People crowded the streets and talked about it. The wounded came limping home to tell their stories of how the Americans had won.

Many of the women of New Orleans went to the battlefield to care for the wounded who could not be brought to the city. Today our armies have field hospitals and trained nurses to care for injured soldiers. Of course there was nothing like that then. After the battle of January 8th, New Orleans women went to Chalmette in carriages, carrying bandages and blankets, fresh clothing and baskets of food. Even the Governor's wife, Mrs. Claiborne, went, as well as Mrs. Edward Livingston. Many of them took their servants with them, and General Jackson later gave special thanks to the work the colored women did among wounded and sick men at Chalmette.

On January 23rd the victorious soldiers came back to New Orleans in triumph. The whole city waited for them. The streets and balconies were crowded. People stood on rooftops. Flags decorated houses and shops and streets. The citizens who had not been able to fight the battles now shouted cheers at the heroes—the tough Kentuckians and Tennesseans, the young Frenchmen, the Baratarians, the Mississippi dragoons, the Negro soldiers.

Dominique You and Beluche rolled their cannons through the streets, Dominique roaring with laughter almost as loud as cannon fire itself. Just behind General Andrew Jackson at the head of the parade rode the Lafitte brothers, Pierre smiling and waving, Jean as quiet as usual, his eyes bright. Now the people of New Orleans shouted praise at him. He was a hero. They were all heroes.

There were speeches and a pageant in the Place d'Armes—the old parade grounds in front of the Cabildo and the St. Louis Cathedral. The Place d'Armes was afterwards named Jackson Square in honor of Andrew Jackson and the Battle of New Orleans. An arch of triumph had been built in the center and the army passed beneath this while cannon boomed and a band played military music. Boys and girls in costume, representing the States of the Union, held flags and ribbons and tossed flowers at the returning men.

General Andrew Jackson was crowned with a laurel wreath. He didn't like that very much for it was not the kind of thing that pleased him, but he let them place the wreath on his head.

Then he took it off. After all he had been called "Old Hickory" for a long time, and he was happier shooting it out with Indians than being fussed over.

That night there was an immense ball. It was the biggest ever held in New Orleans. The whole city tried to get in, and descriptions of it sound as if almost everyone did.

In any case it must have been a strange affair, with all kinds of people there—Creoles and

Americans of all kinds, and the men from Barataria who had been called pirates not long ago. Even Andrew Jackson was persuaded to dance at least once. He danced with his wife, for Mrs. Jackson had arrived in New Orleans not long before. We are told they hopped all over the ballroom floor to "Possum up de Gum Tree," a popular piece of music at the time. The style of dancing was as fast and as much fun then as it can be today.

Streamers across the ballroom floor had large lettering on them which read: "Jackson and Victory: They are but One!" General Jackson looked up and read them and grinned a bit dourly. "Why not 'Hickory and Victory'?" he asked. He had never liked being called "Old Hickory" very much.

Of course we don't know what the Baratarians thought of all this, or even how many of them were there. But the leader of them all certainly was, and he was the most popular man present. Jean Lafitte moved about the huge room surrounded by people who wanted to congratulate and thank him for what he had done for New Orleans. Many of them told him that without his Baratarians the Americans might not have won. As usual Lafitte was quiet and solemn and dignified. These balls were not places where he was happiest, any more than General Jackson was happy at such affairs.

Yet, as always, Lafitte was very popular, especially with the ladies. Afterwards many of them wrote letters to friends about him and about meeting him at the Victory Ball. We can still read these letters and they give us a very good idea of what people thought of him that night. Of course the ladies all remarked about how handsome he was and what fine manners he had, but they wrote of other things, too.

One lady wrote that Lafitte told her "He had never been a pirate, and his only crime was privateering, which he explains by saying he has a deep hatred for Spain, owing to the cruelty which he suffered from the Spanish when confined in a fortress of Havana." That is one of the clues we have to Jean Lafitte's mysterious past, for so far as we know, he told no one else about adventures in Havana.

Another lady wrote, "Mr. Lafitte told my husband that he has long hated the British, owing to their cruel treatment of himself as a young man." There we have another mystery. How many misfortunes had Lafitte suffered before coming to Barataria and New Orleans? Had the British once treated him so badly that he had been anxious to join the Americans in fighting them?

The most exciting moment of the evening came when Governor Claiborne came over to Lafitte with Mrs. Claiborne on his arm. The story is told that Mrs. Claiborne smiled and said, "Mr. Clement!" She remembered the time she had met Lafitte at her friend's plantation and that Lafitte had been introduced to her by that name. She must have remembered how they had spent a long evening talking and laughing together. Some romantic writers say that Lafitte and the Governor's wife then danced together, and it is quite possible, although we do not know if they did or not.

Later in the evening, however, Claiborne and Lafitte were seen talking together in a corner of the room. Those who overheard their conversation said they were joking about the time they had offered rewards for the capture of each other. Everything had changed a lot since then.

The ball lasted nearly all night and it was not until almost the end that one disagreeable thing happened. General Coffee, who was General Jackson's brother-in-law, came over to the corner where Claiborne and Lafitte were still talking. Claiborne introduced Lafitte, but General Coffee did not seem to hear. He turned his head and began saying something to Claiborne. Lafitte took it for an insult. He stepped toward Coffee, his eyes hard and cold.

"Lafitte the pirate!" he said loudly enough to be heard across the room.

General Coffee turned and bowed. Of course, he said. He knew him now. He apologized. He had not heard the Governor and had not meant to be rude.

Lafitte turned and walked away, his quick temper blazing. He never forgot it. He never believed he had not been insulted.

Perhaps he was just tired of the ball. This was not his kind of life. Perhaps he was already planning to escape all this and find a life he liked better.

19: Lafitte Leaves New Orleans

JEAN LAFITTE WAS SEEN EVERYWHERE IN New Orleans during the days that followed. He was often in Governor Claiborne's offices. He was often with his attorneys, John Randolph Grymes and Edward Livingston. He attended a few social affairs, but no more than he could help. As in the old days, before a price had been set on his head, he was seen most often with his brother. He and Pierre strolled the streets together, and sat and talked with gentlemen in the coffee houses.

Of course all the Baratarians were free now and they could go wherever they pleased in the city without danger of arrest. Most of them, however, soon disappeared into their marshes. A few of the lieutenants were always about. Gambi was often seen, but he made people uncomfortable and they avoided him. Nez Coupé was in a different position. He was liked and soon he was talking about going into business in the city. Beluche was around for a while, and then he vanished, probably back into the swamps— at least for a while.

Aside from the Lafittes, the most popular of all the privateers was Dominique You. He was treated as a hero, and everyone liked his laugh and his fierce appearance. This old buccaneer was a good fellow, it was said. A good heart and a fine sense of humor were hidden under his rough exterior. He was a special favorite with Andrew Jackson. At the Victory Ball he had danced with all the ladies, and if he had not danced so well, he had made them all laugh. Besides all this, it was said that Dominique was about to give up his wild ways and settle down.

Meanwhile Jean Lafitte was waiting. He was

pardoned from all the charges against him, as were all his men. But this pardon was not a legal one—it meant only that the citizens had forgiven the Lafittes and their men. There had not been time to make it official, and that was what Jean wanted.

John Grymes and Edward Livingston were at work, however. They wrote letters to President James Madison immediately after the Battle of New Orleans. They asked not only a pardon from the United States Government, but also full American citizenship for all the privateers who had not been Americans before. The lawyers also asked that citizenship be restored to every man who had been a citizen before joining Lafitte's band.

The President's proclamation was not long in coming. It was received less than three weeks after the celebration for American victory had been held. In the proclamation President Madison spoke of the courage with which the Baratarians had defended New Orleans. He mentioned their refusal to help the British even though offered bribes to do so. He declared all those who had taken part in the defense of New

Orleans pardoned of any and all crimes they may have committed before the British invasion. He declared them citizens of the United States.

As proof that they had taken part in the fighting each man had to have a letter signed by Governor Claiborne. These were easily obtained. Claiborne wrote the letters gladly, and it was over. The Baratarians were all American citizens.

Lafitte was glad of this, but he was not satisfied. He still had much to remember, much that kept him from being happy. New Orleans was saved, so he turned his mind to his own problems. His whole life was changed. Grande Terre had been almost destroyed. A large part of his property had been seized by Captain Ross and Commodore Patterson. Those of his ships that had not been sunk had been captured and were still in the hands of American officials. He wanted the return of all that he had lost. He was a man who always fought for what he thought were his rights.

Grymes and Livingston went back to work. They sued for the return of all Lafitte's goods and property. What was in the storehouses of the officials must be returned to Lafitte. The ships that were still tied up at the wharves must be given back. All that had been destroyed, both merchandise and ships, must be paid for in cash.

This was not done, for the officials wanted to keep what they had. They argued that the Baratarians had been pirates at the time the goods and property had been taken from them. To beat Grymes and Livingston all the Lafitte property was put on auction at once. Sauvinet, Lafitte's banker, bought the ships back under his own name, and Lafitte bought them from Sauvinet. He was still a wealthy man.

All this made Jean Lafitte bitter. He thought he had been treated unfairly and that he had been robbed in a certain way. He may have brooded about other things. He was a citizen and most people treated him as an American hero. But he may have asked himself if that would last. He probably remembered what he had considered the insult of General Coffee. More than a year passed and he felt no better.

Not that Grymes and Livingston gave up the struggle for the recovery of the Lafitte treasure. They even sent the District Court of Louisiana all the letters and documents the British had given Jean Lafitte when they had tried to bribe

him. They also gave over the letters Lafitte had
written Blanque when he was trying to get Claiborne's consent to fight for the United States.
But nothing was recovered except the ships
Sauvinet managed to buy back.

Lafitte and his lawyers fought it out all
through 1815 and 1816. Then he began to feel
it was useless, and, as he had feared, some of the
citizens of New Orleans began to be less friendly
than they had been just after the battle at Chalmette. Gossip became common.

When Lafitte started to make more and more
trips to Grande Terre people wanted to know
why. He now owned eight ships, they said, nearly
as many as he had owned before. Was he about
to return to his habits of smuggling and privateering? Had he really been a pirate and was he
about to become one again?

Barataria was now well guarded. Public
opinion was changing. There were few persons
who still thought smuggling was all right. Most
of the people began to think that privateering
was just as unlawful as piracy. The majority of
the men at Barataria were now nothing but
fishermen, but it was said that Lafitte was work-

ing among them, trying to get them to join with him in forming another buccaneer's empire.

In the spring of 1817 Jean Lafitte vanished. He took with him Pierre Lafitte, Dominique You, and a number of Baratarians. They sailed from Grand Isle in his eight ships. For a time no one knew where they had gone.

Of course Lafitte knew exactly what he wanted to do. He was angry and he was bored. He wanted to return to his adventurous life. He and his men sailed the eight ships to Port au Prince on the island of Santo Domingo. They called upon the officials there, hoping to be welcomed. Dominique You was a native of the island; this was his home.

Unhappily, the party was not welcomed. There were too many stories, true or false, about the Lafittes and their crews. Jean and Pierre Lafitte both argued, and Dominique tried to help through powerful citizens of Santo Domingo who were his friends. It was no use. The officials did not want them there. They were told they could not use Port au Prince as a base for whatever business it was they hoped to conduct. They were allowed to restock the ships with food and water, and then forced to leave. So they set their sails to the breeze again, sea rovers once more, feeling homeless.

It was then that the Lafittes decided to go to Galveston on the Texas coast. Here conditions were very much like those that had existed at Barataria a year or two before. Here Jean Lafitte felt he could have a kingdom of his own again.

But Dominique You left them. Somewhere, some time, he had decided he did not want to return to that life. He went back to New Orleans. One day he was seen in the streets again, and everyone said, "There's old Dominique! I told you he was a good fellow. Now he is back to stay." He was back to stay for the rest of his life.

On his way to Galveston Jean Lafitte stopped for a time at Barataria. Here Dominique You parted company with him forever. Lafitte coaxed more Baratarians to rejoin him, and then he was gone once more.

There was still another incident that must have had much to do with Lafitte's leaving New Orleans. Shortly after the Battle of New Orleans a Spanish consul had come to the city. This was to show that the United States and Spain were friends. Lafitte could no longer lead his ships

against Spanish vessels. They were no longer—
by any standards—his rightful prey. He would
again be outlawed by the United States if he
began to attack them as before.

The United States and Great Britain were also
at peace, so he could not war on English ships.

Galveston seemed to offer him more opportunity. In many ways it resembled Barataria.
The Gulf of Mexico would still be his front yard
and he could roam it as he pleased. Too, although Texas was still a part of Mexico, and
Mexico still belonged to Spain, there were men
at Galveston who were fighting for freedom from
Spain. Jean Lafitte went to Galveston to take
over its rule.

If New Orleans ever saw him again—and
there is no proof that it did—it was only for a
brief visit now and then.

View of New Orleans from LAFITTE STREET

20: New Orleans, American City

IT HAS BEEN SAID THAT THE BATTLE OF NEW Orleans should never have been fought at all. In a way this is true. The War of 1812 was over before the struggle took place. A treaty between the United States and Great Britain was signed at Ghent on December 24, 1814. On that day British and American troops faced each other on the plantations below New Orleans. They were to continue fighting for almost another month. It took so long for news to travel in those days neither side knew the war had ended.

Yet the Treaty of Ghent was not ratified until February 15, 1815, so, from another point of view, the war was still going on. There was fighting between Englishmen and Americans as late as February 12th. On that day the British captured Fort Bowyer at Mobile from the Americans.

However, the Battle of New Orleans was not fought in vain. Its success was so complete and spectacular that it had an important effect on Americans all over the country. We had won the war in every way important to us and the treaty with Britain gave the United States nearly everything its representatives at Ghent asked for. Nevertheless, American armed forces had very few military successes. The country needed the victory at New Orleans to lift its spirits. No doubt it gave the British and other European countries something to think about, too.

For New Orleans, the victory was the real beginning of its place as an American city. Until then it had been more French than anything else. Its citizens thought of themselves as anything but Americans. After they had united to fight off British invasion this feeling began to fade.

During the years following the war, more and more Americans came to settle in New Orleans. French and Spanish Creoles began to speak English. They intermarried with English-speaking Americans. Soon the English language was being taught in the schools instead of French. Soon the people of New Orleans were as American as those of any other city in the nation. Of course the coming of many Americans had its part in bringing this about. Yet it was the Battle of New Orleans that had made everyone realize that they were all one people, bound together in one cause.

It is curious that Jean Lafitte and his Baratarians played so large a role in this. Without them the Battle of New Orleans might have been lost. The British had to fight them not only at Chalmette, but all through Barataria. It was the help Lafitte's men gave the forces of the United States in those marshes that was important in driving the enemy from Louisiana.

Jean Lafitte's adventures in Galveston are really another story, but a little about them can be told here.

When the Lafittes' ships sailed into Galveston harbor they found the port almost deserted. Galveston was theirs for the taking. A village was soon built, which Jean Lafitte called Campeachy. There he had a fine house built for himself, which he called Maison Rouge, or Red House, for it was painted bright red. It was half fortress, and cannon jutted out toward the sea from its upper story. Around Lafitte's home his men built many smaller houses for themselves.

Soon recruits began pouring into Campeachy, some of them Baratarians who had once been in Lafitte's band. It was not long before he again had a thousand men under his command. Smuggling was resumed and in no time Jean Lafitte was again being called a pirate. It was just like the old days!

The end of this venture came in 1821, four years after Lafitte had left New Orleans. United States ships entered the harbor and the officers called upon Lafitte. They told him Campeachy had to go. Again Lafitte denied that he was or ever had been a pirate or that he had ever done any damage to American vessels or property. Indeed, he was now an American citizen. Had he not fought for the United States against the English?

The officer in charge, a Lieutenant Kearny, could not be moved. He would order his ship, the *Enterprize,* to destroy the village unless Lafitte and his men left it.

That night Lafitte set fire to Campeachy. Men aboard the *USS Enterprize* saw it burst into flames during the night. When they went ashore at dawn they found only ashes and rubble. The ships of Lafitte were gone, taking with them every living person who had been in the village.

After that Jean Lafitte vanishes into almost as complete a mystery as that which had surrounded him before he appeared in Barataria. There are many stories. Some writers have said that Lafitte and his crews settled in Yucatan off the coast of Mexico and went on with their business for a number of years, and that Lafitte died in Yucatan. He was reported leading a band of pirates operating off the northern coast of South America. Others have said that he settled down to a respectable life in a town in the Middle West, married, raised a family and died quietly in his old age. There are still other stories.

What of the others who played important roles in Jean Lafitte's career and in the winning of the Battle of New Orleans?

Of course Pierre Lafitte vanished with his brother, and there are also many tales about him. It has been said that he died in Yucatan, too, that he was recognized as captain of a ship sailing out of Charleston, that he went to Washington and fought a long time to get back the money the Lafittes thought the Government owed them. We do know he was in Washington for a time, that he made efforts to get the money, but that it was never collected. His end remains just as mysterious as that of his brother.

Dominique You did settle in New Orleans and became a respected citizen. He went into politics and was a well-known figure in the city for many years. When he died he was buried with full military honors, and the inscription on his tomb describes him as "the intrepid hero of a hundred battles on land and sea; who, without fear and without reproach, will one day view, unmoved, the destruction of the world."

Beluche went to Venezuela, carrying a letter of recommendation from General Andrew Jack-

son, and became a commodore in the navy of
that country. He sailed the seas until he died and
is one of the heroes in Venezuelan history.

Gambi, always the bad one, tried to be a pirate
again. He organized a crew of the worst sort of
Baratarians. In the end his own men cut his
throat.

Nez Coupé, or Louis Chighizola, opened a
fruit stand in the French Market in New Orleans.
He lived a long time and loved to tell tales of
the days when he had sailed the Gulf of Mexico

with Jean Lafitte. He has many descendants in New Orleans and throughout Barataria.

We all know, of course, that Andrew Jackson eventually became the president of the United States.

After Jackson was president he appointed Edward Livingston his Secretary of State. Livingston later became ambassador to France and had a long and distinguished career.

William Charles Cole Claiborne died in 1817. Mrs. Claiborne, his widow, then married John Randolph Grymes, who with Livingston had been an attorney for the Lafittes. Grymes was elected to the Louisiana Legislature, and later became United States District Attorney. He grew richer with the years and more powerful. He fought duels and always won, as he almost always won his cases in the courts.

General Humbert, despite his age, went to war at least once more. He fought with the Mexican patriots for the freedom of Mexico from Spain. Then he settled down in New Orleans and became a teacher in a French college for the rest of his life.

That was the way the principal leaders in the

fight to defend New Orleans during the War of 1812 ended. New Orleans has never forgotten them, especially Jean Lafitte. A street in the city is named after him, as is a town in Barataria. People still talk about his exploits and the mystery surrounding him. They visit the places where he lived and had headquarters, from the villages below New Orleans to the blacksmith shop and the other buildings where he had adventures in the old French Quarter of the city.

People still argue about whether or not he was a pirate. They even search the marshes for buried treasure that they never find. It is probable that Lafitte buried none. More likely, he always sold his loot for cash and put the money in Sauvinet's bank.

Pirate or not, no one has forgotten Jean Lafitte or his part in the Battle of New Orleans. Pirate or not, he was also a patriot who helped save the city and for that New Orleans, now completely American, will always remember him with gratitude.